LAHORE
A GLORIOUS HERITAGE

GOLDEN JUBILEE OF PAKISTAN
50 Years
1947-1997

LAHORE
A GLORIOUS HERITAGE

IHSAN H. NADIEM

SANG-E-MEEL PUBLICATIONS
25-Shahrah-e-Pakistan (Lower Mall) Lahore.

954.9143 Ihsan H. Nadiem
        Lahore: A Glorious Heritage /
Ihsan H. Nadiem.-Lahore : Sang-e-
Meel Publications, 2006.
        200pp. : with Photos
        1. .History - Pakistan - Lahore.
I. Title.

2006
Published by:
Niaz Ahmad
Sang-e-Meel Publications,
Lahore.

ISBN 969-35-1807-1

SANG-E-MEEL PUBLICATIONS
25 Shahrah-e-Pakistan (Lower Mall), P.O. Box 997 Lahore-54000 PAKISTAN
Phones: 7220100 - 7228143 - 7667970   **Fax:** 7245101
http://www.sang-e-meel.com e-mail: smp@sang-e-meel.com
Chowk Urdu Bazar Lahore. Pakistan. Phone 7667970
PRINTED AT: MAHMOOD KAMBOH PRINTER, LAHORE.

Dedicated to my family:
Suraiya, Asem, Iram and Asef

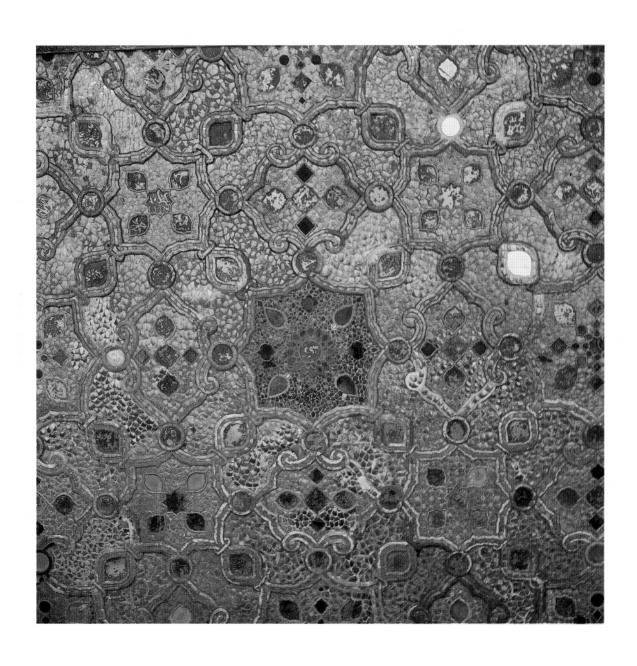

CONTENTS

PREFACE

'Lahore Lahore aey'. Thus goes the popular Panjabi saying that literally means 'Lahore is Lahore'. The expression, however, encompasses a sense much wider in meanings than what is conveyed by these three simple words. It refers to the peculiarity and the particularity of the traditions and traits very strongly identified with the city. Yet another term 'Zinda dilan-e-Lahore' - or the lively Lahorites - only betrays of the pleasant and amicable character of its inhabitants, and speaks volumes, again, of the charm and spell Lahore is capable of casting upon any one.

Going a little farther, there is still another Panjabi adage which tells that those who have not seen Lahore, have not been born. What a tribute to a living city! It, no doubt, is an unambiguous pointer towards the undying appeal Lahore has in it. No wonder then it has always allured not only the fortune hunters, conquerors but also the saintly personages and chroniclers.

Its location on the River Ravi - and on way to Central India - has served long the invaders from north. It was its strategic position, and its being a ready source of replenishment of men and material for the exhausted invading armies, that Sher Shah Suri had wished, only if he had gained time, to destroy it to the extent that it could never be rehabilitated. The intensity of his feelings again indicates the importance he attached to Lahore.

While it is no less than an honour to write on such a city it nevertheless poses a challenge in sifting facts from myths and legends of its past. I have, however, chosen to go for and bank upon the former, but without disregarding the latter. The book is thus expected to be fairly sincere and more direct, and communicative in approach.

In writing this book I have made use of the published material as well as of my own notes prepared at different times from many original or direct sources, and on the basis of my personal study and experience of the remains during many years of association with the physical heritage of Pakistan in general and Lahore in particular. It is pertinent to record here that some of these notes reflect the outcome of intensive discussions with my professional seniors, and even younger colleagues, hence of immense weight and rare value. I am thankful to all those friends for their keen interest in the study of Lahore and for their moral support in the plan to pen down a monograph. The latter aspect was extremely difficult, I must admit, as the required hours to be spared from the official encumbrances were few and far between.

While writing a book on a city with complex and long cultural history it is well nigh impossible to stick to the chronological order of the physical heritage

9

still found above the ground. One finds the architectural remains of different periods overlapping or mixed up with one another, though at times not indistinguishably, at a number of spots. There are quarters where remains of distinctly separate eras are found intermingled in the same while at others a single period is sometimes seen scattered over a vast format. The subject of architectural legacy has, therefore, been dealt only keeping in mind the convenience of the reader, for that matter a visitor to this great city, so that a clear picture comes out without going back and forth. It is hoped that this will help in easy and quick grasp of the past manifestations.

Throughout the book Gregorian calendar has been followed while any deviation is duly mentioned with the letters B.C. standing for Before Christ or A.H. denoting the Hijra era. Similarly the measurements have been referred to in the metric system, at times giving only the standard abbreviations like km for kilometre, m for metre, cm for centimetre etc.

For more serious readers, a select bibliography is given at the end. It may help further the utility of this book.

To bring out the depth of beauty and grandeur of its architectural heritage, liberal use of photographs and drawings has been made. All the illustrative material, unless otherwise mentioned, is my own love's labour, as is also the composing of the whole text on my personal computer.

My earlier books, Moenjodaro: Heritage of Mankind and Rohtas: Formidable Fort of Sher Shah, were well received in the circles of scholars and information-seeking enthusiasts. The next book in that series was planned many years back and, in fact, work had started in early 1995. However, keeping in view the happy occasion of the golden jubilee of Pakistan falling in 1997, it was decided to accelerate the pace of the work and bring out the results well before the onset of the jubilee year. It is just to pay a tribute, in a humble way, to the city which had contributed in a big way in the creation of Muslim ideological state. My publisher friend, Mr. Niaz Ahmad, was only too keen to contribute his share for the honours. I am obliged to him.

At the fag end of the completion of this book Amjad Jawed helped me in re-setting some odd pictures while Hafiz Mohammad Arif and Nazir Ahmad assisted me in bringing in line some drawings. I am thankful to them all. No less I am grateful to Habib Ghani for his untiring help in researching some of the missing links in Lahore Fort's history.

I am grateful to my journalist friend, Rafique Dogar, himself an author of many books, for being readily accessible on phone to discuss many a point that would enhance the usefulness of the undertaking. No less I am indebted to my teacher, Prof. A.H. Dani, for his very positive and encouraging pats which tended to boost morale, so very necessary at quite a few busy junctures of my delivering an obligation. I must also record my appreciative thanks to my wife, Suraiya, for smilingly forbearing my `burning the midnight oil' in working for Lahore'.

104-Umer Block
Allama Iqbal Town
Lahore
August, 1996.

Ihsan H. Nadiem

PROLOGUE

Lahore, the cultural metropolis of Pakistan, is a city where myth and legend are so intertwined that historians and scholars have not yet been able to clearly spell out its true origin and early growth. Its chequered history has seen not only the periods of glory and abundance but also the eras of utter chaos and distress. Throughout its life it has remained the fabled prize of the famous conquerors as also of the notorious warriors.

Although an important city throughout the ages, the genesis of Lahore remains wrapped in a hazy mist of time, only dimly appearing in the folklore. Following the Hindu epic, the *Ramayana*, it is attributed to *Loh* (or *Lava*), a son of the legendary *Rama* or *Ramchandra*, thus implying *Loh-Awar* or the Fort of *Loh*, going back to the remote antiquity making it one of the oldest cities. Mention of a city, commonly identified as Lahore, is also made in connection with a journey of *Megasthenes* the Greek ambassador to the court of *Chandra Gupta Maurya* from 306-298 B.C. He extolled the fortified city of great culture and charm. The chronicles of *Kanishka*, the famous *Gandharvi* king of the *Kushana* dynasty also mention of battles for a city on the banks of the river Ravi, in the second century of the Christian era. In the seventh century the widely acclaimed Buddhist pilgrim from China, *Hsuan Tsang*, recorded his passage through a large city, in all probability Lahore, while on his way to Jullundhar in eastern Punjab.

The very location of Lahore by the banks of the Ravi gives it the prime importance as a centre of defence. Dividing the Indus plains from that of the Gangetic one, it stands on the most frequented eastward route from Central Asia to the heart of South Asian Subcontinent.

11

River Ravi

HISTORY

In the haze of remote history the scanty evidence suggests that for almost ten centuries Rajput dynasties dominated the scene in this region. It was because of their presence that the city of Lahore rose to importance and served as a forerunner of other colonies. Its natural role made it up to the status of the capital of the province.

Like the riddle of its origin and early history, its name has also been a constant topic of discussion without any definitive evidence to suggest as to how it came to be known as Lahore. As mentioned earlier, one of the theories connects it to *Loh*, the son of *Ramchandra*, the hero of the famous Hindu epic *Ramanyana*. It would be interesting to note that a small temple attributed to *Loh* still exists near the western extremities of the present brick-fort, in the north-western side of the old city of Lahore.

Loh Temple

In *Deshwa Bhaga* it is mentioned as *Lavpor*, which points to its having founded by *Lav*, the son of *Ramchandra*, thus corroborating with the myth. In the ancient history of Rajputs it appears as *Loh Kot*, literally meaning 'the fort of *Loh*', in all probability ascribing it to the same legendary founder.

The early Arab geographers also make mention of the city in different ways as at different times. Ahmad *bin* Yahya surnamed *Al-Biladuri*, the author of the famous *'Futuhul Baldan'* believed to be one of the earliest Arab chronicles, calls it by the name of *A`lahwer*. It is frequently cited in the same way by other ancient Arab geographers.

The great Arab traveller of the ninth century of the present era, *Al-Idrisi*, mentions it as *Lohawar*, thus coinciding with the early Hindu legendary accounts. The name has been taken to mean "fort of *Loh*" as the terminus *'awar'* is now taken to be a corruption of Sanskrit word *Awarna*, meaning fort. It thus also recognizes its identity with the *'Loh Kot'* of the Hindu *Puranas* as the word *kot* goes in for the same meaning as *awar*.

In his famous work of the tenth century, *Al Kanun*, Abu Rehan *Al-Biruni* also calls it *Lahawar*. Later French and British writers have, however, read it differently as *Lauhaour, Lohaovar, Loharu, Lahor* etc.

Hazrat Amir Khusrow calls it *Lahanur* while referring to it in his famous work, *Kiranus-Sa'den*, towards the later part of thirteenth century. In the early fourteenth century, Rashid-ud-din, in his book *Jamiut Tawarikh*, mentions this city as *Lahur*.

Although the name of Lahore has been written in many different ways throughout history yet one thing comes out very clearly that in all its variations it kept the essence of the legend referring to the mythical *Loh*, usually taken as its founder.

The foregoing inference may take the origin of Lahore back to pre-Christ era but the first mention of *'Loh Kot'* in ancient Hindu scriptures could be found around the middle of second century A.D. when Prince Kaneckson migrated from here to Dwarica.

At almost the same time Ptolemy, the celebrated astronomer and geographer from Alexandria, makes a mention of a city called *Labokla* situated on the route from Kashmir to Putna. Its location corroborates with other accounts suggesting that the city was no other than Lahore. It could thus have been founded towards the end of the first or beginning of the second century of the Christian era. The theory is further strengthened from the interesting situation that the historians of Alexander the great do not mention any city by the name of Lahore, or by any of its variations, thus hinting at the conclusion that it either did not exist at all or was of no consequence during the fourth century B.C.

Lahore appears to have gained position of prominence in the eighth and ninth centuries when it served as the capital city of the reigning family of *Brahmans* who in the tenth century were attacked and conquered by the Turk Subuktagin and his son Mahmud. However, during these times of invasions it seems to have been mentioned as *Suba* or province. The archaeological excavations in the Lahore Fort in the 1950s have confirmed that a fort did exist here during the times of Mahmud of Ghazna.

Subuktagin, a general and slave of Alaptagin - himself a celebrated Turkish slave and general of Abdul Malik, the last of the *Samani* kings of Bokhara - succeeded to the throne at the death of Alaptagin in 977. He had successfully subjugated and annexed Qandhar before marching on to the kingdom of Lahore, at that time ruled by Hindu *Raja* Jaypal of the ancient lineage. The Hindus were defeated and Mahmud retraced to Ghazni after settling peace for 1,000,000 dirhams and fifty elephants.

The *Raja*, however, not only turned back from paying the *'jaziya'*, the ransom to the Muslim king, but also cast into prison the messenger who had accompanied him to collect the same. His treachery once again brought Subuktagin to the soil of Punjab when the whole country upto the banks of Indus was duly humbled.

At the death of Subuktagin in 997, his son Mahmud ascended the throne of Ghazni, though after a disputed succession. He led successful invasions of India humbling most of the *rajas* and chiefs of the region in order to fulfill his dream of establishing the religion of the Prophet (peace be upon him) on the lands beyond the Indus.

It was in the year 1021, after forbearing a repeatedly treacherous conduct of Jaypal, his son Anangpal, and in turn, his son Jaypal II, that the armies of Mahmud ransacked Lahore when it was permanently annexed to the empire of Ghazni. A regular garrison was thus established first time east of Indus, and the Hindu principality of Lahore ended for ever, laying the foundation of the future Islamic empire in India.

Some of the greatest poets of Persian language, like Abu'l-Faraj Runi (d. 1091) and the other Mas'ud ibn Sa'd Salman (d. ca.1131), whose works were greatly admired throughout the Persian speaking world, belonged to this area.

Still another great personage, Umar al-Jallabi al-Hujwairy, commonly known as Data Ganj Bakhsh, came to Lahore from eastern Iran after wandering through the Islamic world in pursuit of mystical knowledge. His Sufi work, *Kashf-al Mahjub*, 'the Unveiling of the Hidden', being the first treatise on mystical life in the Persian language, has eversince become a source of inspiration for the pious and truth-seekers. After his death around 1072 his tomb became a place of pilgrimage and a centre of spiritual solace not only for the masses but also served as guide to the South Asia subcontinent for other mystics coming from Iran and Turkestan.

The contemporary chroniclers have recorded that Sultan Mahmud built in the fort of Lahore victory tower to commemorate the subjugation of the well-known Hindu temple of *Somnath* in Southern India, in 1025. His slave and governor of Lahore, Ayaz, also added certain buildings here during that period. The successors of Mahmud shifted their court from Ghazni to Lahore when the city became the hub of socio-cultural and political activities. Scores and scores of immigrants from all corners of the Central Asian region came to settle here. The following 165 years saw Lahore being ruled by no less than 15 Ghaznavid Sultans, through their generals and viceroys.

Newly-built mosque, and tomb of Data Ganj Bakhsh

During the reign of Mahmud Ghaznavi Lahore was called Mahmudpur, as is evident from the coins struck by him at Lahore. The numismatic evidence also corroborates with the contemporary chronicles that the Ghazni Sultans were a tolerant lineage and some of them even adopted Hindu titles. They also employed the Hindus in their cavalry and gave them equal opportunity in life.

Shahab-ud-din Muhammad Ghori, brother of the Sultan of Ghor, Sultan Ghias-ud-din, was sent to annex the provinces which belonged to the subverted dynasty of Ghazni. He faced not much difficulty in conquering Multan and Uch but met with very determined resistance from Khusrow Malik that he had to lift siege of Lahore both the times as he tried to subjugate. Changing his strategy, Muhammad Ghori made the prince come out of the Fort of Lahore and thus surrounded him finally to surrender in 1186. The Ghaznavid Prince with all his family was put to death and Lahore occupied soon after without any difficulty.

After having been wounded seriously at the battle of Narain on the Sursuti river, Sultan Shahab-ud-din Ghori was carried to Lahore, almost insensible while his army was defeated and pursued by the Hindu *Raja* of Ajmer. The latter carried his arms to the gates of Lahore for as many as seven times but was finally defeated and put to death by the Sultan in 1193.

Taking advantage of the absence of the Sultan to Khwarazm, the Gakkhars, a valiant tribe inhabiting northern mountainous region of Punjab, not only over-ran the province but also captured Lahore in 1203. However, Shahab-ud-din, with the assistance of his deputy, Qutb-ud-din Aibak, originally a slave, regained Punjab and induced the Gakkhars to embrace Islam.

Tomb of Ayaz

17

It was at Lahore on 24th July, 1206 that after the assassination of Sultan Shahab-ud-din at the hands of Gakkhars, Qutb-ud-din Aibak, already a viceroy of northern India, ascended the throne.

Another of the slaves of Sultan Shahab-ud-din Ghori, Taj-ud-din Eldoz, not only retained the possession of Ghazni and the northern provinces at the time of the death of his master but also set out with an army to enforce his claim over Lahore. He was successful in capturing the city but was soon driven out by Aibak who marched to Lahore at the head of an army from Delhi.

The rule of Sultan Aibak did not last long as he died in Lahore in 1210 through a fall from his horse while playing *chowgan* (or polo) and was buried here.

After Sultan Aibak, his son Aram Shah mounted the throne. But he was soon defeated and expelled from Lahore by the late King's son-in-law and adopted son, Shams-ud-din Altamash. Sultan Altamash appointed his son Nasir-ud-din Mahmud as viceroy of Lahore in the beginning of 1217.

In the following year, Jalal-ud-din, the Sultan of Khowarzm, after subjugating Persia and Transoxania conquered Lahore. His army was, however, driven back to the banks of the Indus by the mighty legions of Chengez Khan.

Sultana Razia Begam succeeded her brother Rukn-ud-din Feroz, the son of Altamash, to the throne of Delhi. Her Governor of Lahore, Malik Azad-ud-din Kabir Khan rose in revolt. The Sultana then led her army from Delhi to Lahore and humbled the chieftain to obedience in 1239.

On the assassination of Sultana Razia in October, 1240 her brother, Sultan Moz-ud-din Behram Shah ascended the throne. It was during his reign that the army of Mughals captured Lahore when the governor had fled to Delhi.

In the following reign of Nasir-ud-din Mahmud as Sultan of Delhi (1246 - 1266) the viceroyalty of Lahore was held by Sher Khan. The latter was successful in repulsing the repeated attacks of Mughal army on Lahore. He was even able to invade their territory and take possession of Ghazni.

Nasir-ud-din Mahmud died in 1266. His *Wazir*, Ghias-ud-din Balban also known by his title as Ulugh Khan who was already exercising powers of the king ascended the throne as Sultan at Delhi.

On the death of Sher Khan around 1270 the Sultan appointed his eldest son, Prince Muhammad as viceroy of Lahore. In the face of repeated excursions of the Mughals from the direction of Sindh, the Prince held his court at Multan.

It was during this time, as the *Tarikh-e-Firoz Shahi* mentions, that the Lahore Fort was ordered to be rebuilt at the orders of the Sultan who had marched to Lahore while returning from one of his expeditions to *Koh-i-Jud* (Salt Range). The author of the treatise, Zia-ud-din Barni speaks about Lahore also as a region when he mentions that *he re-peopled the towns and villages of Lahore, which had been devastated by the Mughals, and appointed architects and superintendents to restore them.*

Tomb of Qutbuddin Aibak

During the successive reigns of Khilji and Tughlaq dynasties, spanning over a period of about 126 years, Lahore does not appear so prominently in the political history of the times. The Mughals continued on sprees of invasions of the surrounding areas. It was during this period that a number of Mughals settled near the town of Lahore, where their inhabitated quarters came to be known as Mughalpura.

Ghazi Khan, the viceroy of Lahore during Ala-ud-din Khilji's times, effectively stopped the incursions of the Mughals. He succeeded even pushing them into Kabul and Ghazni.

Originally the son of a Turk slave of Ghias-ud-din Balban, Ghazi Khan laid the foundation of the ruling dynasty of the Tughlaq kings (1321 - 1414) when he ascended the throne in 1321 under the title of Ghias-ud-din Tughlaq.

During the Taymur's adventure into South Asia in 1398 he over-ran Punjab and Multan but Lahore was saved any pillage due to the timely submission of the Khokhar chief. The latter, however, changed his stance once the Emperor was in Delhi. A detachment was sent to subjugate him, levy and collect contributions and plunder the country. The campaign was a success. The conqueror returned to Turkistan without having established any garrison in Punjab, though appointing Syed Khizr Khan as his viceroy of Lahore and retaining only titular suzerainty over Hindustan.

On the death of Mahmud Tughlaq in 1412, Syed Khizr Khan marched over Delhi and after expelling the former's successor, ascended the throne. During the reign of Syeds for about sixty six years Lahore did not enjoy any place of prominence in the political scenario.

After experiencing a few ups and downs in the affairs of Punjab, Lahore was conquered by Emperor Zaheer-ud-din Babar in 1524. The town was plundered and its streets burnt. The Emperor halted here for only four days and then marched on to Dipalpur. After crossing the Sutlej he had advanced as far as Sirhind when the Lahore affairs necessitated his hastened return to curb the revolt of Dowlat Khan Lodhi. The latter, on hearing of the King's approaching march fled to the nearby hill country on the east. After giving over the charge of Lahore to Mir Abdul Aziz, the Emperor started back to Kabul.

Babar had hardly crossed the Indus when Dowlat Khan, coming from the hill-country, advanced to Dipalpur. The Emperor, on his fifth and last excursion, subjugating the area, without entering Lahore which came well in his control, marched on to Delhi where in Panipat he defeated Ibrahim Lodhi to lay the foundation of Mughal rule in Hindustan. It was on 20th April, 1526.

During the Mughal rule, especially in the reigns of the early Emperors, Lahore once again gained importance and served as a place of royal residence. This period saw it becoming the seat of learning to which were attracted men of letters from places like Bukhara, Samarkand etc. It also witnessed its golden period of material abundance when fine gardens were laid out, remarkable feat in canal digging achieved, spacious mosques built, caravan serais and palaces constructed, thus giving impetus to its architecture unmatched in any age of its long history.

Three days after the death of Babar, his son Humayun ascended the throne in the city of Agra on 29th December, 1530. Kamran, his brother, who held Kabul and Qandhar at that time covertly tried his luck at the throne but could not succeed, even with intrigues, beyond claiming Lahore, and then whole of Punjab as far as Sutlej. The Emperor being of a mild disposition, confirmed his brother in his government of Kabul, Qandhar and Punjab.

After his defeat at Kannauj at the hands of Sher Shah Suri, Emperor Humayun fled with his brothers Hindal and Askeri and sought refuge at Lahore. As Kamran had made peace with Sher Shah by ceding Punjab to him, Humayun, with the imperial family, was compelled to quit and cross the Ravi on 31st October, 1540. The Mirza separated from the Emperor near Hazara and His Majesty proceeded to Sindh in search of help to regain his lost empire.

Sher Shah Suri who had pursued the Emperor from Agra, through Punjab, laid the foundation of a fort at Rohtas in the Gakkhar areas to meet any eventuality should Humayun join hands with his brothers and try his luck again.

In January, 1555 Humayun crossed the Indus after an exile of over fourteen years. He met with no resistance and entered Lahore. After making appointments for the administration of the city and the province of Punjab, he marched on to Sirhind.

Kamran's Baradari

On the death of Humayun in 1556, his son Jalal-ud-din Akbar who was then only thirteen, ascended the throne. He was at the time encamped at Kalanor during an excursion against Sikander Shah Suri. After his accession, the first important event that Lahore witnessed was the capture, and then escape, of its Governor, Shah Abu'l Ma'ali.

The Emperor arrived at Lahore during the second year of his reign and stayed here for four months and fourteen days. It was during this time that one of his ablest administrators of the later years, Abdul Rahim *Khan-e-Khanan*, was born at Lahore in the house of his tutor and famous General, Bairam Khan.

Akbar marched to Lahore against his half-brother, Muhammad Hakim Mirza, who in a bid to establish himself at Lahore, had caused some disturbance. The Mirza fled even before the Emperor had arrived. His Majesty entered Lahore, the *Dar-us-Saltanat*, and put up in the house of Mahdi Qasam Khan in the fort.

The Emperor went out, around Lahore, for a great hunt in the early part of 1567. After having enjoyed the festivities of the game for several days he returned to the city. He started his march back to Agra on 22nd March, 1567, leaving the affairs of Punjab in the hands of Mir Muhammad Khan *Atkas*.

Akbar visited Lahore in the fourteenth year of reign, after paying his homage at the shrine of Baba Farid Shakar Ganj at Pakpattan (Ajudhan).

After his victorious march on Kabul in 1579 the Emperor held feasts and great rejoicing in the capital of Punjab on his return journey. The *Daulat Khana-e-Aam*, or the Halls of Public Audience, which consisted of one hundred and fourteen porticos, was especially decorated for the festivities. Akbar marched towards Fatehpur in the following year.

In the thirty-fourth regnal year, when Akbar went to Kashmir, he left Todar Mal Khatri, the famous financier and revenue accountant, in charge of Lahore. Todar Mal had been raised to the rank of *Wazir* of the empire in the twenty-second year of the reign of Akbar and was made governor of Punjab after he was given the rank of Seven Thousand. He died in Lahore in 1581. In the following year also in Lahore died Urfi, the great poet of Akbar's court.

Akbar made Lahore his headquarters for fourteen years, from 1584 to 1598. It was from here that he conducted his military operations against Kashmir, planned wars with north-eastern Afghans, undertook the conquest of Sindh and Qandhar and managed his campaigns against the Yousafzais.

The Emperor Akbar married his son, Prince Saleem, to the daughter of Rai Singh at Lahore in the thirty-first year of his reign.

Akbar seemed to have developed notions of religious liberality during his long stay at Lahore. He also erected two buildings outside the city for feeding poor Hindus and Muslims, one of which he called *Dharampura* and other *Khairpura*. At a later stage a separate receiving-house was added for *jogis*, and given the name of *Jogipura*.

Akbar revived the old Persian festival of *Nauroz* in honour of the sun, which he adored at the time of its rising when he appeared daily in the *Jharoka*, or balcony window, of the palace to be worshipped as an embodiment of the deity.

The Emperor's partiality was not confined to any particular religion. He was courteous to the Christians as well. At the earnest request of the Emperor, the Portuguese government at Goa sent missionaries to his court at Lahore, in 1595. Their hopes, however, did not realize and they eventually left for Goa. His son and successor, Jahangir, was more liberal. He allowed Portuguese Jesuits to establish a mission and build a church and school at Lahore. He also appointed stipend for the priests. Shahjahan, Emperor Jahangir's son and successor, being a strict Muslim stopped these pensions and demolished the church.

Lahore was also visited around 1584 by four Englishmen -Newbury, Fitch, Storey and Leeds - members of a company in Turkey. It was also here on 5th October, 1595 that a jewel of Akbar's court, Faizi died.

Prince Saleem ascended the throne at Agra in 1606, and assumed the title of Jahangir. Six months later, his eldest son, Khusrow, broke into open

Diwan-e-Aam, Lahore Fort

rebellion and fled to Lahore, to which he laid siege. The Prince was over-powered and brought to the court in fetters. His life was spared but the rebel grandees and the army espousing with Khusrow were eliminated after horrible punishment.

The fourth Sikh Guru, Guru Arjan, was placed in confinement at Lahore, for conspiring against the Emperor in the same rebellion. He died of rigours of imprisonment, though his followers attribute his extinction to a miracle.

Jahangir was fond of Lahore, and held his court here on his way to Kabul and Kashmir. In the following year he was met here by the Amirs of Iraq and Khorasan, the envoy of Persia, and the agent of the Sharif of Makka.

In the fifth regnal year Jahangir appointed Sheikh Farid Bokhari as governor of Punjab. He built at Lahore a *mohallah* after his name, a large bath and a *chowk*, or square.

In the fourteenth year of his reign, His Majesty ordered to be built a minaret known as *Kos Minar* at every *kos* (a measure of distance), and a well at every three *kos* from Agra to Lahore, on the grand trunk road.

In the year 1621 the Emperor entered Lahore, after hunt at Jahangirabad (Sheikhupura) and 'put up in the edifices which had been newly built under the management of Ma'mur Khan'.

In the fifteenth year of his reign, Emperor Jahangir visited the new palace of Prince Khurram. Lahore also witnessed great rejoicing the same year when the son of Prince Shahr Yar, the fifth son of the Emperor, was married to the daughter of Nurjahan by Ali Quli Beg.

In the twenty-second year of his reign, the Emperor fell ill in Kashmir. He was on his way to Lahore when he died at Rajauri in 1628. In accordance with his will, his body was sent to Lahore and buried in the garden of Nurjahan.

Sultan (Prince) Khurram, the son of Emperor Jahangir, was born at Lahore in 1592. He was nominated in 1616 by his father as successor and awarded the title of Shahjahan, when he was also made the commander-in-chief of the army of Deccan. He thus had special affiliation with Lahore and incidentally much of the drama of his accession to the throne also took place here. The machinations of the widowed Empress Nurjahan to install at the throne her son-in-law, Prince Shahr Yar, who was married to her daughter Mehr-un-Nisa by Sher Afgan, did not succeed in the end. Shahjahan was proclaimed Emperor at Lahore. The rebels who had taken up with the cause of Shahr Yar were all put to death. Nurjahan, the widow of Jahangir was, however, granted an allowance of two lakhs of rupees per annum.

The royal *Harem* of the Emperor remained in the palace of Lahore until the fourth regnal year. According to *Badshahnama* of Mulla Abdul Hameed Lahori, the carpet manufactory of Lahore was established by Shahjahan in the sixth year of his reign.

After his ascending the throne, Shahjahan held his court at Lahore in 1628 when Hakim Ilm-ud-din surnamed Wazir Khan, was the viceroy of

Punjab. During the same visit His Majesty ordered him the reconstruction of *Ghusal Khana* and *Khwabgah* (bathrooms and sleeping chambers) and complete the work by the return of the Emperor from Kashmir. He also ordered dismantling and rebuilding of *Shah Burj* (royal tower), execution of which was left to the taste of Yamin-ud-daula Asif Khan.

Shahjahan held his court again in Lahore in 1631. About this time Qandhar which had been in possession of the Persians since the seventeenth regnal year of Jahangir, was surrendered to the Emperor by its viceroy, Ali Mardan Khan, who was then appointed to the governor-ship of Kashmir.

Lahore at this time was at the height of its splendour and glory. Like the Emperor, many of the *Omra* and grandees added jewels of building art. It was at this time that Lahore was also visited by envoys of foreign nations, among them were the *Amir* of Balkh, the *Wali* of Turan, the Safavi King of Persia and the sovereign of Basra.

The court remained at Lahore in 1635 when the Emperor's fourth son, Murad Bakhsh, was betrothed with the daughter of Shah Nawaz Khan *Safavi* and was sent to Multan as governor. The same year, the Emperor graced the newly completed gardens, the *Farah Bakhsh* and the *Faiz Bakhsh*, jointly known as the *Shalamar*. Towards the end of the year, the royal court moved to Agra.

In 1638 Shahjahan again visited Lahore but marched on to Kashmir after halting in the gardens of *Farah Bakhsh* and *Faiz Bakhsh*. The Emperor returned to Lahore the same year and held the court here for the next two years.

Nurjahan died in 1638 at Lahore and was buried in the mausoleum built by herself in her lifetime.

The premier noble of Emperor Shahjahan, Ali Mardan Khan died in 1675, on way to Kashmir. His body was brought to Lahore and buried here.

The eldest son of Shahjahan, Dara Shikoh, was fond of Lahore and adorned it with many beautiful buildings and spacious *chowks*, or squares. On the contrary, Aurangzeb, Shahjahan's other son, mostly remained busy in fighting protracted wars in the Deccan and had less time to hold his court at Lahore, though it continued to be called as *Dar-ul-Sultanat* in public correspondence.

In the war of succession, Dara Shikoh after his defeat at Agra at the hands of Aurangzeb, marched to Lahore and, after taking possession of the citadel, seized royal treasury and began raising an army. Aurangzeb after settling firmly at Delhi marched to Lahore in pursuit of his brother. Unable to resist Aurangzeb's pressure, Dara Shikoh fled to Multan with gold and silver treasures. Aurangzeb leaving his eldest son, Prince Muhammad Azim, in charge of Lahore marched to Multan but Dara had already fled to Bhakkar. The Emperor Aurangzeb Alamgir then came to Lahore where he reached on 24th of Moharram 1069 A.H. (1659) and put up in the Shalamar Gardens. The next day he inspected the fort of Lahore.

Dara Shikoh proceeded to Ajmer, when his faithful wife, Nadira Begam died. Her corpse was sent to Lahore and buried, according to her will, in the precincts of the mausoleum of Mian Mir.

Aurangzeb visited Lahore in 1656 and stayed in *Faiz Bakhsh* (Shalamar) for two days before entering the city at an auspicious moment. The next day he asked his Friday prayers in the mosque of Firoz Khan outside the Fort, near to the Hathipol Gate. He also received at Lahore envoys of many friendly countries.

In 1662, Lahore was much damaged by the excesses of the Ravi. The emperor caused to be built a massive embankment of brick work for about four *kos* along its left bank to save the city from its encroachments. Not only that the city was saved from turning into ruins but the course of the river was also pushed towards north, further away from the city.

The court was held at Lahore during the years 1668 and 69, when the Emperor also visited Hasan Abdal and other places on the frontiers, and then

Kos Minar

26

stayed in Kashmir. On his return, the Emperor camped in the Garden of *Dilkusha* across the river Ravi for a few days. A grand *Darbar* was then held in the *Shah Burj* of the Lahore Fort.

In the twenty-third year of the reign Prince Muhammad Azim was appointed Viceroy of Punjab. However, a few years later, in 1694, Sultan Muhammad Mu'azzam - afterwards Shah Alam - replaced him as Viceroy.

After the death of Aurangzeb Alamgir the brilliant period of Lahore, as that of the Mughal empire, came to an end. The Viceroy of Lahore assumed semi-independent position while the Sikhs began to rise as an independent entity, fast becoming a threat to the peace of the country.

Aurangzeb left behind many children but none of them could achieve the height of their past glory. The Mughal dynasty lasted for another century but their internal strifes, legacy of violence and incompetence of the successors reduced them into titular body with less and less control over its provinces which started increasingly attaining autonomous status. This anarchic condition was just ripe to open the doors of South Asia for the two great conquerors who over-ran the area which had been the domain of the Mughals for over two centuries. The first was the Persian ruler and a legendary Asian warrior, Nadir Quli known in history as Nadir Shah who, while withdrawing from India took with him the famous Peacock Throne, a symbol of Mughal power. The second was his Afghan successor, Ahmad Shah Durrani Abdali. Both of them would bring years of bloody wars and savage onslaught to

Jahangir Tomb Sarcophagus

Diwan-e-Khas-o-Aam: View from North-west (Jahangir's Quadrangle)

Lahore. Together, in a period of about thirty years (1738-1767) they invaded and captured Lahore for no less than nine times, at the end, leaving behind only a shattered populace and a vulnerable empire, never to regain for Mughals a comprehensive control over their territory.

With the weakening of the Muslim power in Delhi, and the internal intrigues at the court of Lahore, Sikhs in the meanwhile assumed an organized martial appearance and continued to disturb peace. They held power over Lahore for short spells of time but were no match to the invaders from the north. Ahmad Shah, however, confirmed Lahore in possession of Bhangi *Sirdar*, Lahna Singh, before retiring to Kabul after his eighth - and final - invasion.

For the following thirty years Lahore experienced relative calm under the triumvirate of Sikh rulers: Lahna Singh, Sobha Singh and Gujar Singh, and their three sons who took over in turn. But in 1797, Shah Zaman , the grandson of Ahmad Shah Abdali, once again invaded Lahore. He, however, soon returned to Kabul because of a rebellion back at home.

In the following year, Shah Zaman again marched at Lahore. This time too his immediate return to Kabul was necessitated by the unstable circumstances. But before returning he formally bestowed the chief-ship of

Wazir Khan's Hammam: Interior of the dome:
(Photo courtesy Ian Harper)

Lahore on Ranjit Singh for the services rendered by him to the Durrani monarch, especially by retrieving and dispatching to Kabul eight out of twelve heavy guns which had sunk in the river Jhelum.

Ranjit Singh had no special affection for the old triumvirate which in any way had grown much weaker. Through sheer cleverness, and chivalry, Ranjit Singh occupied Lahore as conqueror, while the last of the triumvirs fled.

Although Ranjit Singh never took the traditional string of titles usually granted to a Maharaja, nor did he stamp his name on the coins that he issued, yet in 1801 in a grand *Darbar* he assumed the title of *Sirkar*. signifying 'state'.

The new kingdom of Lahore was growing larger with Ranjit Singh's recent acquisitions when in 1808 he, breaking off negotiations with the British emissary - Thomas Metcalfe - attacked them south of the Sutlej. As the forces on the British side moved, with help of native Sirhindi chiefs, the Maharaja

Wazir Khan's Mosque General View.

30

Shalamar Garden: Marble throne and Central Tank with Mahtabi and
two pavilions of second terrace. Third terrace also seen.

Tomb of Hazrat Mian Meer

preferred to make peace and acceded to their demand to leave the country east of the Sutlej alone. In the bargain Ranjit Singh was left free to expand boundaries of his 'empire' to the north and west. It gave the opportunity to the British to consolidate their *Raj* east of the Sutlej while Ranjit Singh's empire extended to include Multan, Peshawar, Kashmir, Kabul and Derajat. At the time of his death in 1839, at the age of 57, he also left behind a disciplined army of over 80,000 troops, and a well-knit whole of various chieftains.

Ranjit Singh was succeeded by his son, a dull Kharrak Singh, who ruled for only one year and four months. His son, Naunihal Singh, though a capable heir, lost his life on the very day of coronation. He was returning from the funeral of his father when an archway of the Roshnai Gate crashed on him and killed him.

A struggle for power ensued between Chand Kaur, the widow of Kharrak Singh and mother of Naunihal Singh, and Sher Singh, the dubious son of Ranjit Singh. Sher Singh succeeded in taking over power after an honourable compromise with Chand Kaur. He, however, was killed three years later, as a result of a conspiracy in which his young son, Prince Pratab, was also assassinated alongwith Dhian Singh, a minister of Ranjit Singh and a trusted supporter of Sher Singh.

The intrigue for power never stopped afterwards. Dhian's son, Hira, took revenge and became *Wazir* as Dalip - another son of the late Maharaja Ranjit

Refugees Under the shadow of Badshahi Mosque 1947.
(Photo courtesy F.E. Chaudhry)

33

Singh - took the throne. Hira was also eliminated as Rani Jindan, Dalip's mother, came to an influential position. She helped hasten the end of the Sikh rule with her secret collusion with the British who routed and completely destroyed the Sikh army. Immensely pleased with their acquisition of the Sikh territory, they even occupied Lahore in 1846, keeping Dalip Singh as the nominal ruler. However, by 1848 he was also deposed quietly and exiled to the English country-side where he lived on the pension of 50,000 Pounds Sterling per year.

In 1849, while Bahadur Shah Zafar, the last of the Mughal dynasty, sat impotently in Delhi, and the deposed Sikh Maharaja Dalip Singh thousands of miles away in England, the British East India Company was able to establish a new over-riding ruling body and thus began the century of British rule in India till 14th August, 1947, when the Subcontinent won its independence and alongwith Bharat an independent Islamic State of Pakistan appeared on the map. Lahore became the capital of the province of Punjab and continue to serve as the cultural metropolis of the country.

Quaid-e-Azam's address in Badshahi Mosque, 1938.
(Photo courtesy F.E. Chaudhry)

Minar-e-Pakistan

An arieal view of Lahore city
(Photo courtesy Ian Harper)

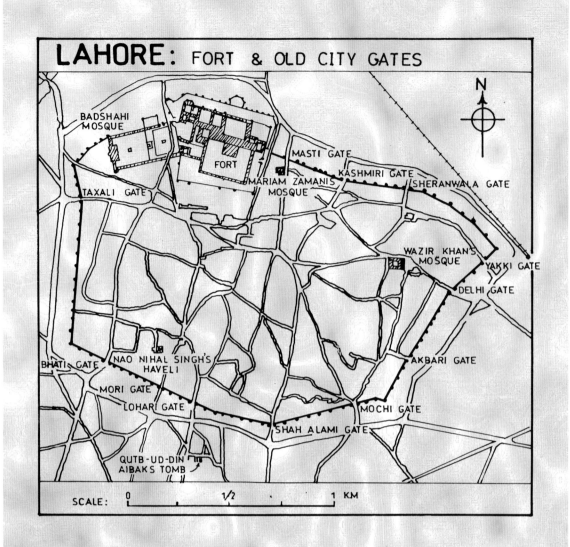

LAHORE: FORT & OLD CITY GATES

N

BADSHAHI MOSQUE

FORT

MASTI GATE

KASHMIRI GATE

SHERANWALA GATE

MARIAM ZAMANIS MOSQUE

TAXALI GATE

WAZIR KHAN'S MOSQUE

YAKKI GATE

DELHI GATE

AKBARI GATE

BHATI GATE

NAO NIHAL SINGH'S HAVELI

MORI GATE

LOHARI GATE

MOCHI GATE

SHAH ALAMI GATE

QUTB-UD-DIN AIBAKS TOMB

SCALE: 0 ½ 1 KM

THE WALLED CITY

Lahore which for some times in history also stood for the name of a province, long served as capital of a vast Punjab. After the partition of the Province at the time of independence on 14th August 1947, it continued to serve as the headquarters of the western part which came to Pakistan. The city is situated in latitude 34° 34'5" N and longitude 74° 21'E, while its height from mean sea level is about 217 metres.

The old, walled city is in the shape of a parallelogram, with the imposing Fort carved out in its north-western corner. In ancient times the river Ravi, the smallest of the five rivers giving Punjab its name, used to flow along the northern wall of the city and the fort. As the river, notorious for its changing course, rolled on towards further north away from the city, the Fort was extended mainly for defence. The Ravi floods, however, posed threat to the city and, at least for once, its encroachments caused so much alarm that in 1662 the Emperor Aurangzeb Alamgir made an huge embankment of bricks and mortar along its left bank, running for about six kilometres, and thus saved the city from the mass destruction. The Ravi further changed its course and is presently flowing about two to three kilometres north of the old city. The old course of the river, or the *buddha* Ravi as is locally known, has either been usurped for habitation or given to large and beautiful parks where Minar-e-Pakistan now stands.

The city perhaps saw its worst period when, during the successive rules of Hindu kings, it was deserted due to civil wars. It was re-populated by Sultan Mahmud Ghazanvi at the time of invasion of the country and conquest of Punjab in 1021. His slave and confidant, Malik Ayaz who was left here in charge of the garrison established by the Sultan, enlarged the town as also the citadel. He died here and lies buried in one of the quarters of the city.

The archaeological excavations carried out in 1958 in the south eastern part of the present Fort of Lahore yielded, among other things, a gold coin of Sultan Mahmud of Ghazna, portraying the period of its abundance at its earlier stages.

Emperor Akbar during his fourteen years' stay at Lahore (1584 to 1598) enclosed the fort with a brick wall to serve as fortification. He also founded palace buildings, which activity continued throughout the golden period of the Mughals as his successors enlarged and added to the construction towards north and west to the citadel.

39

A model of the Old City, 19th century
(copy courtesy Ian Harper.)

Maharaja Ranjit Singh rebuilt portions of the wall, added a moat and fortification, especially on northern side, mainly to make good the weakness in defence due to shifting of the river Ravi. The ditch has since given way to parks and gardens while the military character of the wall south of the Fort was changed by the British for fear of its re-use against them.

The old, or walled, city is over two kilometres in length and above one kilometre in breadth, which also includes the fort in its north-western corner. The historic city has a circumference of almost seven kilometres where a wall interspersed by thirteen gates runs majestically.

The building activity did not limit itself to the confines of the city wall even during the long historic period of its existence. Many palaces, pleasures gardens, living quarters, tombs and mosque were constructed in the near, or a little far, suburbs of the city. The British added systematically by constructing a huge *chhowani* or cantonment towards south of the main city. The modern population pressure has resulted in the spilling-over of the city and its expanding on all the four directions. The main thrust is, however, on the south where the new colonies, housing schemes and other development projects have extended Lahore upto Raiwind, a town about 40 kilometres away from the walled city.

The old and walled city had effectively controlled accesses. It could be entered through thirteen gateways, provided in the huge wall at intervals throughout its peripheral run. The gateways were differently named. Starting from the north-western corner they were:-

1.   *Roshnai darwaza*, or the 'gate of lights', lies between the *Badshahi* Mosque and the Fort. As it was most frequented by the royalty, *Omra* and courtiers, it was profusely lit up at night hence the name.

2.   *Masti darwaza*. The name of the gate is the corrupt form of *Masjidi* (of the mosque) or more appropriately *Masiti*, as the mosque is known in Punjabi language. It is called so as it faces the famous Maryam Zamani Mosque.

3.   Kashmiri *darwaza*, was named as such as it opened in the direction of Kashmir.

4.   *Khizri* or *Sheranwala darwaza*. As the river Ravi used to flow lose to the city on this side, where ferry was located, the place was known as *Khizri* after Khizr, the patron Saint of waters and discoverer of '*aab-e-hayat*' the elixir - or water of immortality. However, during the Sikh period, Maharaja Ranjit Singh kept two domesticated lions at this gate, which gave it the popular name of *Sheranwala darwaza* or 'lions' gate'.

5.   *Yakki darwaza*. It is the corrupt shape of "Zaki", named after the saint who was martyred here while fighting against the Mughal forces.

6.   *Delhi darwaza*, named so as it opened on to the trunk road to Delhi.

7.   *Akbari darwaza*. It is named after the Emperor Akbar who had rebuilt the city and its fort with burnt bricks. A market close to it, said to have been built during the same period, still flourishes as *Akbari mandi*.

8.   *Mochi darwaza*. The name *mochi* (though meaning cobbler) seems to have originally been *moti* or pearl, named after an officer of Akbar, Moti Ram who resided in the quarters close to here.

9.   *Shah Alami darwaza*, named after Muhammad Mu'azzam Shah Alam, the son and successor of Aurangzeb Alamgir, opened towards south. The gate having become the victim of 'modernisation' and the so-called development of the area, has since disappeared leaving only the legacy of its name.

Roshnai Gate

Masti Gate

Kashmiri Gate

Sheranwala Gate

City wall near Sheranwala Gate

10. *Lahori darwaza*, also commonly called *Lohari* (pertaining to blacksmith), was named after the city itself. Most probably the quarters of the city first populated during the period of Ayaz, were around this gate.

11. *Mori darwaza*. As the name *mori* or hole implies, it is the smallest of all the gates and is said to have served as refuse disposal route of the city.

12. *Bhati darwaza* is called after the name of the Rajput tribe which inhabited the area in ancient times.

13. *Taxali darwaza*, seems to have been named as such as *taxal*, or mints, of the Muslim period rulers were located in this area.

46

Delhi Gate

Lohari Gate

Bhati Gate

Following the ups and downs of history the city of Lahore also had its share of abundance and chaos. The ancient city was not just confined to the old wall but covered a much larger area, which fact is manifest from the presence of old tombs, mosques, gardens etc. outside and away from the walled city. The old chroniclers have extolled Lahore in their accounts of the city. Thornton speaks of thirty-six *guzars* or quarters of the city and its circuit covering upto even twenty two kilometres during its golden period of Shahjahan's reign.

St.Thomas Herbert in his book on Travels, 1595, speaks high of its climate, trade, city quarters *serais* etc.

A'in-e-Akbari written in the sixteenth century by Abul Fazl mentions it as a magnificent city that has 'few equals'. It also mentions of the building activity undertaken here by the Emperor Akbar, and of more than one thousand shawl manufactories.

Two English traders, Richard Still and John Crowther, visited Lahore in 1626 during the reign of Jahangir. They praise the city and mention it as an important trade centre.

48

A Spanish monk by the name of Fra Sebastian Monrique, who came to Lahore in 1641 during the reign of Shahjahan, gives a vivid picture of the life in the streets and bazaars. According to him it was rather over-populous and there was so much crowding in the streets that the monk had to change the route. He, however, speaks high of the peace and tranquility, and the just manner in which business and trade was conducted. The abundance and the riches manifest from its bazaars and gardens and palaces are eulogized by this traveller.

Another merchant, from France, John Baptista Taverier who travelled from Isphahan to Delhi via Qandhar, Kabul and Lahore during 1641-68 (the reigns of Shahjahan and Alamgir) also mentions of the over population in the city, and of the changing course of the river Ravi and of the riches of the street, which would equal those of the European mart.

Another French traveller, Francis Bernier who passed through Lahore in 1664 notices 'the magnificence of its citadel, thronging of its streets and markets and loftiness of its houses'. But the traveller Thevenot who visited it a year later, in 1665, talks about the start of a decaying process as he saw dilapidated condition of its suburbs.

With the decline of Mughal power started the civil wars at Delhi. Punjab was thus left independent as the seat of the empire could not wield effective control over it. The hordes of militant Sikhs made the best of the situation. The suburbs of Lahore, once rich and populous, were the easy prey and first to suffer. The later wars of succession following the death of Maharaja Ranjit Singh played havoc with the old city and its environs. In addition to these armed conflicts the Sikhs in power also committed acts of depredation and spoliation and were responsible for destroying or damaging many an old building once forming jewels of the city.

The colonial period or the *Raj* saw expansion of the city with cantonment and new quarters of habitation getting developed away from the walled city, which in fact never saw the past glory.

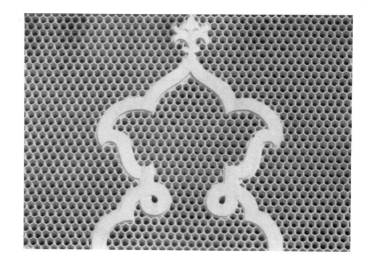

Zam Zama Cannon

ARCHITECTURAL HERITAGE

The physical and architectural heritage of Lahore can generally be divided into two broad periods. The first one may be called Pre-Muslim or Hindu period while the second one would include the long era starting with the advent of Islam in this part of the Sub-continent. The later Sikh period, though not a continuation of the Mughal architectural times or style, mostly thrived on the material skills of their predecessors. The buildings and structures of this period could thus not forge ahead any specific merit or legacy. The Sikhs mostly remained contented with erecting not-too-pretentious *Havelis* or some odd buildings in addition to effecting alterations to the Mughal monuments. Still later period, the *Raj*, brought in influence of an alien civilization and though adapted to the local conditions, could not find favour with the masses, or even elite, beyond a very limited circle. As neither of these later periods of Sikhs and British represent spectacular edifices, and perhaps are still over-awed by the Islamic grandeur, these have failed to identify themselves with the character that stands for Lahore.

Pictured wall, Lahore Fort.

HINDU PERIOD

The Hindu period remains are mostly conspicuous by their absence. The main reason for it could be the use of mud or mudbricks in that remote past, while the frequent invasions and resultant destruction of the city must also have contributed largely to that end. Another factor reflective of its poorness in its architectural remains of Hindu period is manifest from the fact that Lahore had never enjoyed a status of the place attracting Hindu devotees who would build religious edifices of lasting nature.

There are hardly a few places going back to Hindu period. Even those few which could be counted on fingers, are reckoned from tradition rather than presence of physical or architectural remains worthy of mention. The most noticeable among them is the *Loh Mandir* or temple of *Loh*.

Situated near the Alamgiri Gate inside the Old Fort, the temple is a small shrine still supporting the legend of *Loh* the mythical prince, with which the founding of the city of Lahore is attributed. It, however, does not pretend to have any architectural significance, and whatever structure is present it goes back to the Sikh period in the first half of the nineteenth century.

The other places traditionally ascribed to the Hindu period are *Bhairon ka than* and *Chand raat* in the vicinity of Ichhra - then habitational quarters some four kilometres away - and the remains of a *Dharamsala* relatively closer to the walled city.

Loh Temple

MUSLIM PERIOD

The Muslim domination of Punjab starts with Mahmud of Ghazna's invasion and ransacking of Lahore in the year 1021. The following Muslim rule over the area extends almost uninterrupted upto about 1798-99 with the installation of Ranjit Singh in the seat of Chiefship of Lahore.

On the basis of the architectural styles as evident from the remains, this long period of Muslim influence can be further divided into two distinct groups viz. the Pathan and the Mughal. The former, with its pronounced characteristics of using over-lapped arches and the great slope and extensive thickness of wall, may span over the period starting from 1030 upto 1526 or the advent of the Mughal rule. It is, however, a matter of disappointment that, for certain factors of the long history, not many monuments of the period are now found in Lahore. The only architectural remains worthy of mention are those of the *Niwin masjid* and the *Sheranwali Masjid* both of which, though stripped off much of their originality, are works of great solidity, with massive sloping walls.

Niwin Masjid (Low-level mosque)

MUGHAL ERA

The Mughals brought with them a refined taste of architecture and landscaping. The city of Lahore immensely owes not only to the successive Mughal Emperors but also to their *Omra* and courtiers for their keen sensibility to the beauties of nature which is vividly incarnated in the shape of palaces, pleasure gardens, *Havelis* or mansions, mosques, tombs and mausolea. In fact Lahore is now predominantly a Mughal city as far as the architectural heritage is concerned.

The essential features in the architecture of the Mughal period are the overlapping arches, high and bold domes, tall and standing-out minarets and substantial vaulted roofs. Its earlier period, upto the reign of Jahangir, is mainly characterised by ornamentation, consisting of tessellated or mosaic patterns in stone of various colours, or in glazed tiles. The main feature of the second phase or the golden period of Mughal architecture, representing the periods of Shahjahan and his successor, that makes it distinct from the other, consists of the extensive use of the glazed tiles both on the inside and outside of the buildings, while the other decorating technique of colouring employed especially in stucco medallions and arabesque traceries is also found to be in vogue extensively.

The founder of the Mughal dynastic rule in India, Zaheer-ud-din Babar, in his *Tuzk* writes not-very-kind words about the climate, fruits, agricultural produce etc. of *Hindustan.* Not only that, he records a very low opinion about its people and society in general. He also laments about the absence of ice and cold water. It was only but natural for a man and warrior who was born and brought up in a far more delightful and charming region of the valley of Farghana abounding in natural scenery, hills, rivulets, dense foliage and green meadows.

As the Mughals began consolidating their power in India it became imperative for them to create life and atmosphere conducive to their own style of living. This impulse acted as vehicle to give birth to some of the master-pieces of building art and pleasant land-scaping.

KAMRAN'S BARADARI

During the short span of rule of Babar (1526 - 1530) and eventful though broken reign of his son and successor, Humayun (1530 - 1540 and 1555 - 1556), Lahore did not get much share by way of Mughal cultural enrichment in the shape of architectural legacy. The only monument of the period, worthy of mention, is the *Baradari* - or pavilion - of Kamran, a son of Babar and brother of Humayun. On ascending throne in 1530, Humayun conferred on him the government of Kabul, Qandhar and Ghazni. Through a covert planning Kamran also captured Lahore and subsequently the whole of Punjab, to which the Emperor conceded.

Mirza Kamran enjoyed power in Punjab between 1530 and 1540. During this period he laid out a spacious garden with a palace in it. The garden was provided with brick-paved paths, brick-lined water channels and water tanks with fountains. In the centre of the garden he built a *Baradari* or pavilion which in itself was a piece of architectural adornment and a beauty spot for the recreation of the royal house-hold and close friends. Almost during the same period the *Omra* built their own gardens around that of Mirza Kamran's. This development activity made to turn the whole landscape into a picturesque area.

Kamran's Baradari, A view of the Veranda

Kamran's palace and the garden served over two hundred years (1540-1740) as the summer house and recreational spot for the Mughal emperors and princes. It also witnessed some of the events moulding history. It was here that the rebel son of Jahangir, Khusrow, was brought into the presence of the Emperor.

The pavilion was originally a simple brick-built structure, a portion of it rose to double-storey height, and measured over 25 square metres, with five multi-cusped arched openings on each side. The low arches had somewhat prominent haunches, a feature still continuing from the pre-Mughal Muslim architecture.

The central arch was over 5 metres in width while the corner and middle ones were about 3.6 and 2.75 metres respectively. The building which was about 6.4 metres high comprised a big central octagonal room, about 7.5 x 7.5m, around which eight more rooms were symmetrically arranged. A stair-case leading to the middle storey and roof of the *Baradari* was provided in the room on the south eastern corner. The centre of the roof was occupied by a platform about 14.5 x 14.5 x 0.70 m. This block of nine rooms was surrounded by an arched veranda with a width of a little over four metres.

Kamran's Baradari: A General view after Restoration.

56

The whole structure was finished with plaster on the exterior as well as the interior. It was decorated simply in colour especially at the dado.

The river Ravi, on the right bank of which the pleasant landscape was created by the Mirza and other *Omra*, has always been known for changing its course. As it gradually moved away from the Lahore Fort, on its left bank, it caused the citadel extend towards north. But this behaviour of the river had been telling badly on the gardens and pavilions on its opposite side. During the reign of Muhammad Shah, between 1719 and 1748, a major change in the course of Ravi is noted. It wiped out most of the gardens and houses built by Mughal *Omra* in the vicinity of Kamran's garden. The palace and garden of Mirza Kamran shared with them the same fate though the *Baradari* built by him withstood the ravages of water. It perhaps had to succumb to the devastation by the river when it was thrusting against it in the early 60s. In order to save what was left of the monument a cut was made on the northern side of the *Baradari* area, to reduce the pressure of the water. It was thus turned into an island. To save the monument from further erosion and the undermining of the river, the *island* was protected against the currents by stone-pitching held in place by means of wirenets.

The *Baradari* had, however, not been able to withstand the onslaught of the river in the whole process and a portion of it had thus given way.

Kamran's Baradari. Causeway is seen in the foreground.

57

In the early British period the *Baradari* was used as the residence for the European Superintendent incharge of the boat bridge laid on the river Ravi. It was later converted as PWD rest house. Finally it was opened to public as an antiquity.

In order to carry out thorough conservation of the monument to save it from further decay, the Department of Archaeology, Government of Pakistan, had prepared a plan in the early 80s. However, the Lahore Development Authority was assigned the job. Their enthusiasm has resulted in over-restoration which though makes the building, and the area, look much impressive, has robbed it much of its authenticity - the keyword in professional conservation.

Kamran's Baradari: Canal with row of fountains, and flanked by pavements.

OLD FORT

The old Fort of Lahore, generally known by the simple nomenclature of Lahore Fort, stands out prominently amongst the best accomplishments in the architectural history of the South Asian Subcontinent. It is a unique ensemble of Mughal period monuments representing, in a continuous chain, the different phases of evolution of the building art from the Emperor Akbar the Great (1556 - 1605) to the Emperor Aurangzeb Alamgir (1658 - 1707). The later rulers, the Sikhs and then the British also contributed to the legacy, even though in the form of insignificant structures, often mutilating earlier master-pieces through unmindful additions and alterations, and despoliation of the precious decorative and building material to re-use according to their requirement and taste.

The Fort is perfectly carved out in the north western corner of the old city of Lahore. Its location on the high mound with a massive fortification wall separating it from the old city, and the river Ravi washing its northern limits, gave it an independent entity. The shift in the river course necessitated the addition of the defence wall on its north, during the Sikh rule. The further receding of the Ravi, away from the Fort towards north, in fact left just the most suitable ground for laying in its vicinity the Iqbal Park and the Minar-e-Pakistan in the twentieth century.

Although approachable from eastern and southern directions, the Fort is now entered from the western side using the imposing Alamgiri Gate and the unpretentious Postern, cut in the Sikh fortification during the British period.

In the absence of any definite records the theories of the origin of Lahore Fort are based on conjectures and scanty archaeological evidence. It is generally believed that the Fort came into existence with the founding of the city itself. The hero of the famous epic *Ramayana*, a mythic Prince *Loh*, is generally given the credit in this respect. However, limited excavations carried out in 1959 revealed the remains of five distinct periods namely the Hindu, Sultanate/Ghaznavid, Mughal, Sikh and British in the same chronological order.

Its recorded accounts begin with its capture in 1021 by Sultan Mahmud of Ghazna. After going through a number of ups and downs of history the Fort, like the city, entered its golden age with the arrival of the Mughals in the South Asian Subcontinent. The first two rulers of the dynasty, Babar and Humayun, did not leave any mark on the Lahore Fort. However, their successors not only contributed a great deal to the buildings but also extended it during their respective reigns.

The earlier period mud-fort was demolished by Emperor Akbar and rebuilt in burnt bricks, around 1566. It appears that the mud fort was rectangle in shape and occupied the south-eastern part of the present Fort, with its northward extent to the *Diwan-e-Aam*. The Fort, being at a considerable height than the river Ravi and the intervening uneven area on the north, could only be extended if the same level were attained. The Emperor Akbar constructed here basement chambers which rather offered three-fold advantage of bringing the area in level with the existing fort, providing additional usable space and, most of all, offering stability to the super-structures. The successive Mughal rulers further expanded the fort employing the same technique with the result that

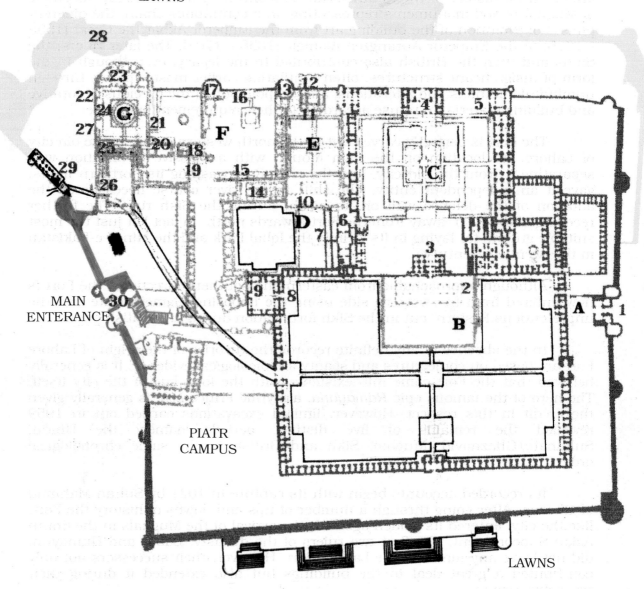

LAWNS

28

23
22
17
16   13   12
24 G   11   4   5
27   21
F
E
20   18
25   19
C
29   26   15
14
10
D   6
7
3
MAIN
ENTERANCE   30   9   8   2
B
A   1

PIATR
CAMPUS

LAWNS

L E G E N D

⬛ AKBAR & JAHANGIR (1556-1627)

⬛ SHAH JAHAN & AURANGZEB (1628-1707)

⬛ SIKH PERIOD (1765-1849)

⬛ BRITISH PERIOD (1849-1947)

almost half of the fort covering the northern portion has rows of such chambers running all along.

An imposing fortification wall runs round the fort. However, much of its southern portion was demolished and replaced with brick-stairs by the British for political reasons before it was handed over as a monument to the Department of Archaeology in 1927. The wall, constructed in different periods following the expansion of the Fort, and shifting of the course of the river on its north, is built in small burnt-bricks and strengthened with semi-circular bastions at regular intervals.

The citadel now contains over thirty different buildings and structures of varying degrees of importance and usefulness, and of course representing different eras of its history.

The Fort can roughly be divided into six blocks or quadrangles in addition to Shah Burj Complex, south-western segment and the moat on the northern side. Almost all the mentionable buildings are situated within these divisions. These areas and their important buildings are as follows:-

A. Akbar's Quadrangle:

It is a vast court occupying the south-eastern area of the Fort. Most of the buildings have now disappeared, partly demolished by Emperor Jahangir to build his *Daulat Khana-e-Khas-o-Aam* and partly by Shahjahan to erect the huge pillared hall of the *Diwan-e-Aam.* Many odd buildings or hutment structures had sprung up for official use during its occupation by army in the days of the *Raj.* These, out of place mushroom of structures, were mostly removed by the Department of Archaeology to restore the original shape of the what-ever-left of the antiquity of the Fort.

1. *Masti* Gate:

The only perfectly surviving building in this Quadrangle is the Akbar's period imposing Gate which opens on the east. The gate is named as *Masjidi* (of the mosque) or more commonly, *Masiti* (from the Punjabi word for mosque, *masit*) and corrupted to *Masti.* It is called so because it faces the famous

Mosque of Maryam Zamani, the mother of Jahangir. The Gate is an huge building, very bold in character, linked by two heavy bastions with battlements and machicolations to add to its military character.

The brick foundations of the buildings of Akbar's period, and demolished in the later eras, could still be seen appearing from the ground at quite a few places.

B. *Diwan-e-Aam* Quadrangle:

It is a vast court which was originally enclosed by a range of vaulted chambers with central gateways. The apartments unfortunately have not survived and since been replaced with plants and shrubs. The surviving buildings in this quadrangle are as follows:-

Diwan-e-Aam Quadrangle.

2. *Diwan-e-Aam* (Hall of Common Audience):

It stands almost in the middle of the northern part of the Quadrangle. Built in red sandstone, it consists of an open hall of forty pillars (*chahl satun*). It was built by Shahjahan in 1631-32, in front of the *Daulat Khana-e-Khas-o-Aam* of Emperor Akbar.

Although very few particulars of the buildings of Akbar and Jahangir in the Lahore Fort are found in chronicles yet detailed accounts of Shahjahan's works easily found help in reconstructing the original set up. He had ordered in the first year of his reign the construction of a hall of forty pillars - came to be known as *Diwan-e-Aam* - in the forts at Agra and Lahore. The *Badshah Nama* of Mulla Abdul Hameed Lahori, the court Chronicler of the Emperor Shahjahan, gives vivid details about its construction for protection from rain and heat of courtiers 'gaining the fortune of admittance and of interview' in front of the *Jharoka* or the royal balcony. Earlier a portico of cloth used to have been erected for the purpose.

The building suffered immensely and perhaps collapsed during the Sikh war of succession around 1841. It was reconstructed during the British period making a random use of the red sandstone pillars, but replacing the whole roof. The building was extensively used by the British as field hospital when the throne-hall of Shahjahan was turned into barracks. The outer archways were bricked up and the building enclosed within a veranda. These excrescence were removed in the early part of twentieth century, exposing the structures which presented the skeleton of the old glory.

Diwan-e-Aam: General View

63

Diwan-e-Aam: General View of Jharoka.

Diwan-e-Aam: A closer view of Jharoka.

3. Daulat Khana-e-Khas-o-Aam:

The oldest of the known buildings of the Mughals in Lahore Fort is *Daulat Khana-e-Khas-o-Aam* built by Akbar. It was here that His Majesty Akbar celebrated the *Nauruz* on 29th December, 1587. The building is recorded to have 114 rooms and bays or aiwans. The *Jharoka*, where king used to appear to give audience to the public was a marble balcony with twelve rooms on its back. There were cells on east and west of the *Jharoka*, with gates for entrance.

Flanking the throne balcony - *Jharoka* - is a long narrow passage, blocked at intervals by partition walls, but running the whole length of the hall on to which it opens at places between the pillars. According to Vogel a little careful demolition of these partition walls clearly showed that before the erection of the great hall an arcade of richly painted columns and brackets formed the main feature of the façade, in the centre of which was the *Jharoka*. When the hall was added, the bays against which the back row of half columns and brackets formed the main feature were filled up to support them. The continuity of the arcade was thus broken. At some later period, the lateral thrust of the arches being feared, the partition walls were built and iron ties embedded in them for strength.

The nobles used to stand in the hall according to their ranks. The presence of the fragments of marble railing still remaining at the site suggests that it must have been used for nobles of some rank to stand here. There were silver enclosures for high ranking nobles.

The red sandstone railing enclosing the raised platform still exists partially. The feature is though absent from the *Diwan-e-Aam* at Delhi and at

Diwan-e-Khas-o-Aam view from Jahangir's Quadrangle.

65

Agra. The said railing was running un-interrupted in front of the *Jharoka*, which feature suggests that the entrance must have been from the sides.

During the reign of Maharaja Ranjit Singh the Hall of Common Audience was renamed and was known as *Takht* or Throne (room). J.P.Vogel mentions that Faqir Qamr-ud-din told him that the Maharaja never seated himself on the imprerial throne, out of respect for the ancient rulers. This well corroborates with other historians who tell us that although Ranjit Singh had commenced his career as a sovereign, he never assumed royal titles, or aspired to regal dignity.

It was here that Chet Singh, the rival of the Minister Dhyan Singh was murdered. The corpse of Maharaja Ranjit Singh was also kept here in state before it was taken to the place where his *Smadh* now stands.

Though the *Diwan-e-Aam* in its present condition does not portray the grace and beauty of Mughal architecture yet its association with historical events still lends it great interest.

C. Jahangir's Quadrangle:

On the north of the *Daulat Khana-e-Khas-o-Aam* lies the expansive Quadrangle. Its construction was started by Emperor Akbar but was completed by his son and successor, Jahangir, in 1617-18 when the final touches were given by the latter's architect, Abdul Karim Ma'mur Khan. This palace was visited by Shahjahan in 1619 and by Jahangir in 1620, when it was highly praised.

Jahangir's Quadrangle: Barri Khawb Gah and Seh Dari in the back.

Although the buildings here did not escape later additions, the greater part of the construction between Akbar's *Daulat Khana-e-Khas-o-Aam* and the river front on the north date from Jahangir's reign.

The buildings in the Jahangir's Quadrangle combine the local brick architecture in the style of Agra and Fatehpur Sikri in the form of sandstone verandas. The *Chhajjas* (eaves) of the *Dalans* were supported by stone brackets in the shape of elephants, felines, lions, peacocks, etc.

The southern side of the Quadrangle also had a row of *Dalans* like the eastern or western side. It is quite evident from the surviving eastern portion while the rest of it is clearly showing in building remains scattered over the area. The habitable portions of these *Dalans* now serve as an archaeological library and offices for garden and conservation staff.

The centre of the Quadrangle is occupied by a garden in the *Charbagh* style with spacious water tank having a square *Mahtabi* (platform) in the middle. The existence of this garden during Mughal period is testified by the description of German traveller Captain Leopold Von Orlich who visited the Lahore Palace in January, 1843, during the short reign of Sher Singh.

The Quadrangle suffered much additions and alterations especially in the open spaces of the garden. Many cook-houses sprung up as also was laid a tennis court during the early days of the *Raj*. Thus the central tank and walk-ways were all covered when the Fort was handed over to the Department of Archaeology to be preserved as a monument.

Another View of Jahangir's Quadrangle

Jahangir's Quadrangle: Red Sandstone columns and brackets, A closer look.

The superfluous structures were removed by the archaeological conservationists. The whole area was completely excavated to expose all the features of a garden. It thus revealed a square tank with 32 fountains in the middle of an elaborate system of pathways which divide the area into a series of garden plots.

4. *Barri Khwabgah:*

Belonging to Emperor Jahangir the *Barri Khwabgah* or the large Sleeping Chamber, occupies the middle of the northern side of the Quadrangle, its back on to the river front. The frontage of the building is the British period reconstruction while the rest of it is in its original layout. The building as a whole, at present, does not portray any architectural feature of mentionable significance.

The building now houses the Mughal gallery displaying the Mughal period miniature paintings, coins, manuscripts, *Framin* or royal decrees, etc.

Barri Khwabgah view from Diwan-e-Khas-o-Aam.

5. *Seh dari:*

On the eastern side of the *Barri Khwabgah* is the *Seh dari,* a pavilion called so because it has three (*seh)* doors (*dar).* Its architectural style suggests its origin in the Sikh period. It is decorated with fresco paintings and is said to have served as an office of Faqir Syed Noor-ud-din, the trusted governor of Maharaja Ranjit Singh.

The frescoes portray floral designs, birds and scenes based on Hindu religious themes and very obviously belong to the Sikh period.

To the west of the *Barri Khwabgah,* there was a similar pavilion demolished probably during the early period of the *Raj.* Its presence could be made out from the remains of the foundations on the ground, though hardly distinguishable, or having been marked on the old map of the Sikh period. It was, though, in this pavilion that Dilip Singh, the last Sikh Raja of Punjab, was born.

A view of Seh Dari.

6. *Shahi Hammam:*

The room situated in the south-western corner of Jahangir's Quadrangle was used as *Shahi Hammam* or the Royal Bath, during the Mughal period. It continued to serve as such during the Sikh reign when it was embellished with colour paintings and beautiful frescoes. The British, however, concealed all the decorations when they plastered the whole place to use it as a kitchen. Some of the frescoes depicting floral designs and female figures along with angels were uncovered during the restoration works of 1950s and 60s.

D. Moti Masjid Quadrangle:

The Quadrangle located west of the Jahangir's Quadrangle, and south of that of Shahjahan's, is known after the tiny mosque of surpassing beauty. The whole enclosure is separated from the Jahangir's Quadrangle with a huge building known as *Dalan-e-Sang-e-Surkh*. The other buildings in this Quadrangle are the *Makatib Khana* on the south and the *Dalans* bordering on the west.

The open court in the middle is divided into two part. The eastern portion which is on the higher terrace, is a spacious platform having brick-on-edge pavement with geometric pattern. In the middle of the platform there is the usual shallow water basin with floral ornamentation, and having a fountain in the centre. The lower part now consists of small garden. It has now been turned into Public Utility Area and houses the restaurant, souvenir shops and public toilets.

7. *Dalan-e-Sang-e-Surkh:*

Against the brick-paved platform mentioned above, is a closed *dalan* of considerable dimensions. It has three arched openings blended with red sandstone screens. The main entrance at present is from the north through a comparatively small door-opening. The entire surface has been treated with deeply recessed panels of various shapes and sizes. Internally, the space has been divided into a central big hall flanked by smaller rooms.

The upper two storeys were added by the Sikh Maharaja Ranjit Singh for his wife, Rani Jindan after whose name it is now also known as *Rani Jindan's Haveli.* The approach to the upper storeys has been provided through a staircase in the southern room.

The building now serves as Mughal and Sikh galleries as part of the Lahore Fort Museum.

8. *Makatib Khana:*

The building with high gates situated on the southern side of the Quadrangle, adjoining the *Moti Masjid,* served as the entrance to Jahangir's Palace (*Daulat Khana*). It was known as *Makatib Khana* or Clerk's Quarters where the clerks regulated the entry to the Palace.

The massive Entrance has a central arched opening towards east. It faces an open courtyard, square on plan and having oblong vaulted chambers

Dalan-e-Sang-e-Surkh.

Eastern view of Makatib Khana

72

on the east, west and north. Yet another high arched-way leads to the main court of the *Moti Masjid* Quadrangle on its north.

A Persian inscription fixed on the façade of the vestibule tells that the palace was built under the orders of the Emperor Jahangir in the year A.H.1027 (1617) under the superintendence of the architect Ma'mur Khan. The inscription which is carved in exquisite *Nasta'liq* characters on a marble slab reads as:

بسال دو از دہم از جلوس مقدس بندگان عالیحضرت شہنشاہ ظل اللہ
سلیمان جاہ کیومرث بارگاہ سکند رسپاہ، خلافت پناہ نورالدین جہانگیر
بادشاہ ابن جلال الدین اکبر بادشاہ غازی مطابق سال ہزار و بیست و
ہفت ہجری عمارت این دولت خانہ ہمایوں با تمام کمترین مریدان و
غلامان فدوی معمور خان صورت اتمام پذیرفت ؛

Its English translation goes as:

> *In the twelfth of the blessed accession of His Imperial Majesty, the shadow of God, a Solomon in dignity, Kayumars in state, an Alexander in arms, the asylum of the Khilafat Emperor Nur ud din, son of Emperor Jalal ud din, Champion of the faith, corresponding with 1027, the building of the auspicious was completed under the superintendence of most humble disciple and slave, the devoted servant, Ma'mur Khan.*

9. *Moti Masjid*:

The mosque wholly built in chaste white marble and attached to the *Makatib Khana* is called as *Moti Masjid*. It is known as such because of the fact that its shiny white domes look like pearls (*Moti*).

The date of the construction of the Mosque is not known with any precision. However, taking into consideration its contemporaneity with the Jahangir's Palace, and the silence of Shahjahan's historians, it is generally ascribed to the former. Henry Cope also mentions of another inscription which should place it in the twelfth year of the reign of Jahangir. As the inscription is found missing, some scholars tend to doubt its authenticity. They, on the other hand prefer to place it in the period of Shahjahan mainly on the basis of its architectural style and merits of decorative motifs.

It is generally taken as the fore-runner of other mosques known as *Moti Masjid* built in Agra Fort by Shahjahan, in Delhi Fort by Aurangzeb Alamgir and at Miharavli or Old Delhi by Shah Alam Bahadur Shah.

During their rule in Punjab the Sikhs converted the *Moti Masjid* into government treasury. The central archway was bricked up and closed with an iron gate, while the remaining four openings were totally closed by erecting brick walls. The building also came to be known as *Moti Mandir* during that period as is evident from the British period records.

73

Moti Masjid

E. Shahjahan's Quadrangle:

Immediately west of the Jahangir's Quadrangle is located an open court enclosed with buildings of the period of Shahjahan on all the four sides. It is thus known as Shahjahan's Quadrangle wherein are located some of the most beautiful palaces manifest of the pinnacle of the Mughal art of architecture. The buildings in this Quadrangle include the *Diwan-e-Khas* on the north and Shahjahan's Sleeping Chambers on the south. The open courtyard in-between these buildings has been designed on the formal *Charbagh* style by dividing it into four by means of walkways, with a square-shaped platform serving as *Mahtabi* in the centre. The raised platform has a shallow cistern in the centre while a fountain occupies the central place in it.

The buildings of the period of Shahjahan are designed in vaulted roofs, multi-cusped arches and carved marble screens. They are mostly in white marble enriched with colourful *pietra dura*, inlays and tessellation.

74

Diwan-e-Khas Quadrangle.

10. *Khwabgah-e-Shahjahani:*

Located between the Quadrangles of *Moti Masjid* and that of Shahjahan, at the southern end of the Shahjahan's Court is the palatial building known as *Khwabgah-e-Shahjahani* or the Sleeping Chambers of Shahjahan. It is also mentioned as *Chhoti Khwabgah* or the Smaller Sleeping Chambers, to distinguish it from the Sleeping Chambers of Jahangir or *Barri* (larger) *Khwabgah* in the Jahangir's Quadrangle mentioned earlier.

The *Khwabgah* has five spacious rooms, the front of which had grand multi-cusped arched openings. The projecting portico on the northern side has been cut off now leaving only the foundations of the walls though the fountain in the cistern still remains at the central place. A small cistern with a fountain also occupies the central place in the Chamber immediately behind it.

The back openings of the Chambers were provided with latticed screens of marble, while the interior was treated with glazed lime plaster with recesses and deep panels of various sizes. The floor and the wall upto the dado level were provided with marble facing. The vaulted roofs had been embellished with stucco tracery as were the walls, which had been covered with thick plaster and new decorations during the Sikh period.

The Department of Archaeology, Pakistan, through sheer luck, caused to expose the earlier period evidence during conservation operations. The fresco paintings belonging to the Sikh period were covered under several layers of white-wash of the British days. These have also been recovered by removing, carefully, the super-imposing layers.

The most striking among the revealed paintings is the fresco depicting a typical Sikh Prince, sitting in a British-style chair, while his consort, on oriental-styled chair offers him a cup of wine. The setting appears to be that of a pavilion on the first terrace of the Shalamar Garden with the trees of the second terrace in the background. A peacock and a few other birds depicted near the couple complete the mood of the scene.

In the second room of the same building, a number of wall decorations in fresco and gold have been uncovered on removing the British period plaster and white-wash.

The frescoes exposed in the third room depict scenes from Hindu mythology. The gaudy colour scheme suggests that they typically belong to the Sikh period.

Sikh Fresco recovered in Khwabgah-e-Shahjahani

11. *Diwan-e-Khas:*

Situated in the northern part of the Shahjahan's Quadrangle, the *Diwan-e-Khas* or the Hall of Special Audience is an arcaded pavilion built in chaste marble in 1645 by Emperor Shahjahan. It is almost square on plan having a flat roof which has a parapet with marble-facing decorated with

76

A marble-screen of Diwan-e-Khas

gracefully delicate border of *pietra dura*. The marble bracketed eave (*chhajja*) surmounted with a parapet is decorated with colourful inlay.

It is supported on five rows of five pillars carrying scalloped arches. The interior is paved with variegated marble. The centre is occupied by a fountain-basin scalloped out and inlaid with semi-precious stones. Most of the inlay has, however, disappeared.

The northern side of the pavilion is enclosed with latticed marble screens with a small window opening in the centre of each screen.

The building served as a military church during its occupation by the British, when in 1904-5 it was taken into pieces and reconstructed.

Diwan-e-Khas: Tank with fountain in the foreground.

12. *Arz Gah:*

Looking down from the *Diwan-e-Khas*, at the foot of the Fort wall we find an old structure of considerable dimensions. It was the place where *Omra* or nobles of the royal court assembled in the morning to receive the Emperor's commands. In the Sikh period map it is mentioned as *Arz Gah* though British travellers refer to it as the *Arz Begi* which term denotes an officer who would read letters and petitions to the king.

While staying in the fort, the Emperor used to sit near the northern screens of the *Diwan-e-Khas* showing his face through the opening each morning to the people gathered together below near the *Arz Gah*, as the *Arz Begis* received petitions from the needy ones.

The building is connected with the Shahjahan's Quadrangle by means of two winding staircases in the thickness of the wall, each opening into the towers flanking the *Diwan-e-Khas* on its east and west.

13. *Lal Burj :*

The *Lal Burj* or the Red Tower occupies the north-western corner of Shahjahan's Quadrangle. It comprises of three storeys, the first having been built during the Jahangir's, the second in Shahjahan's and the uppermost during Sikh period.

F. *Pa'een Bagh* Quadrangle:

Adjoining the Shahjahan's Quadrangle, lying immediately west of it, is a relatively smaller quadrangle. The petite garden and the buildings in this area were effected during the period of Shahjahan. The *Hammams* (Baths), *Pa'een Bagh* (Side or Ladies' Garden), a tank, *Kala Burj* (Black Tower), *Khil'at Khana* and a *Zanana Masjid* (Ladies' Mosque) are among the physical accomplishments located in this enclosure which was meant for the exclusive use of the ladies of the *Harem.*

14. *Hammam-e-Shahi:*

Immediately west of the *Chhoti Khwabgah,* or the Shahjahan's Sleeping Chambers, lies the *Hammam-e-Shahi* or the Royal Bath. It occupies the south eastern corner of the *Pa'een Bagh* Quadrangle, adjoining the *Moti Masjid Quadrangle* on its southern side. The *Ghuslkhana* (Bathroom) as it is also mentioned in some of the contemporary works, was built in 1633 alongwith the Sleeping Chambers of Shahjahan. The superintendence of these buildings was assigned to Wazir Khan by the Emperor.

The *Hammam-e-Shahi* is a single storey structure, symmetrically designed on the longitudinal axis. In plan, it is a double bath as two different sets for men and women have been provided. Reserved for the Emperor it is accessible from the Royal Sleeping Chambers. It contains three main apartments. A vaulted passage runs on the northern side of these apartments. It is connected with the first and second apartments through two entrances while for the third one there is only one such access.

The passage turns and divides into two passages which open on south towards the *Moti Masjid.* The apartment adjoining Shahjahan's Sleeping Chambers, now mostly in ruins, was known as *Jamakhana* or the Dressing and Undressing Room. The *Jamakhana* has one square room at each of the four corners. The royal entrance passes through the north eastern room. These rooms were used for keeping royal clothes and refreshments.

An arched entrance leads into the second apartment of the Bath. Here in the centre is a square tank under the dome. A passage with flat roof runs around the tank which could be used for hot or cold baths. A recess in the southern wall suggests the presence of a couch for the reposing of the *Shahenshah.*

The third or the western-most apartment is a three-bay spacious hall built in north-south direction. There is a room on each of its south-western and north-western corners. To the west of the central bay is a water reservoir with a furnace beneath it. The rooms on either side of the reservoir are connected with metallic feeding pipes for carrying hot water from the reservoir.

The room on the north-western side, with a portion of its floor raised, served as *Baitulkhila* or toilet for the Emperor.

Hammam-e-Shahi

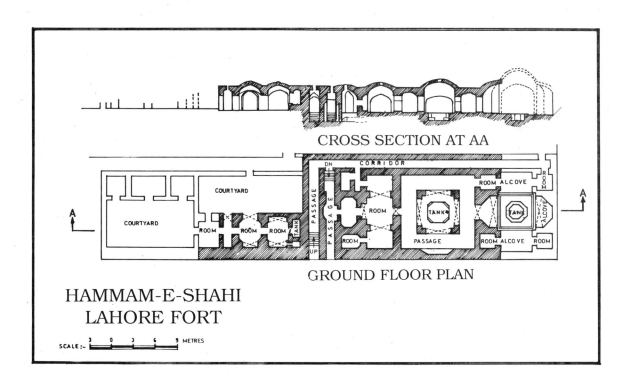

CROSS SECTION AT AA

GROUND FLOOR PLAN

HAMMAM-E-SHAHI
LAHORE FORT

SCALE:-   3   0   3   6   9 METRES

The western part of the *Hammam-e-Shahi* was reserved for the ladies of the *Harem* as it lies close to the Ladies' Quarters and is separated from the eastern one by a partition wall in the vaulted passage.

The water supplied to the Royal Baths came from the well, located on the southern side of the *Makatib Khana*, with the help of a Persian-wheel, and a water-channel used to convey it all the way to the Baths. The traces of the aqueduct are still found over the façade wall of the rooms between *Moti Masjid* and *Shahi Hammam*. The water from reservoir was supplied to different apartments of the Royal Bath by means of terracotta pipe imbedded in the walls.

The whole building appears to be without ornamentation except some rectangular and arched panels with pointed borders found in some of the rooms.

15. *Pa'een Bagh:*

On the northern side of *Hammam-e-Shahi* lies a small though beautiful garden. Known as *Pa'een Bagh* or Ladies Garden, it was reserved for the rest and recreation of the ladies of the royal *Harem.* It is on the pattern of an

Pa'een Bagh Quadrangele: Khil'at Khana

81

enclosed garden having a corridor or gallery running on its four sides. The opening had red sandstone pillars surmounted by capitals and entablatures in the trebeate style. They must have been provided with brick-vaulted roofs. All these elements are now missing, leaving only the remains to tell of their past glory.

In the open courtyard, forming the garden, are arranged a number of square platforms having fountains. The alternate spaces are filled with sweet-scenting plants.

16. *Khil'at Khana:*

A small door opening from the garden area leads to the adjoining second court which has a small but elegant curvilinear pavilion on the north. A deep tank with a fountain is set in the centre, in front of the pavilion which in turn is flanked by other apartments and porticoes on its east and west. It had rich marble veneering of which it was stripped off by the Sikhs.

This small building is known as *Khil'at Khana* because it was here that the nobles and ambassadors were invested with robes of honour or *Khil'at.* The *Bangla*-roofed pavilion is the Hall of Perfumes or *Khas Khana.*

The large chambers in the basement of the Fort in this area can be approached from the east and west of this court.

17. *Kala Burj:*

The *Kala Burj,* literally meaning Black Tower, is a residential building projecting in the shape of half octagon from the northern façade of the Fort. It was towards this side, on to the river front, that the palace buildings originally looked.

The date of the construction of the *Burj* is not mentioned by the historians but a study of its architectural features especially vaults would easily place it sometime around 1610, immediately preceding the *Maryam Zamani* Mosque. The typical vault of the tower well represents the early Mughal style with flat saucer dome sitting on an identical network of intersecting arched ribs that integrate the arches of the transition zone.

The name *Kala Burj* is traditionally ascribed to the times of the Sikhs, as also the upper portion of the tower, which is said to have been built by Jawahar Singh, a brother of *Mai* Jindan, a favourite consort of Maharaja Ranjit Singh.

The central room of the tower, a vaulted chamber nearly 7 metres high is not octagonal, though it appears so outwardly. On the contrary it makes a perfect square measuring 6m x 6m.

The vault is profusely decorated with fresco paintings. The representation consists of birds in the star that form the knots of the network, angels in the fan-shaped compartments arranged in circles, and fighting simuraghs (mythical Persian birds) in the central medallion. The facets that enframe these figurative paintings are filled with arabesques, flowers and flowery ornaments. The subject of these paintings is considered by some scholars to be representing *Hazrat* Suleman (King Solomon) who was the master of the seen and the unseen worlds, and was controlling genies and fairies. The theme may thus be referring to the power and popularity of the great Mughals.

18. Ladies' Mosque:

In the south-west corner of the *Khil'at Khana* Square is located a small building with a *Mihrab,* or niche, in the western wall. Once it was a pretty little mosque used by the ladies of the *Harem.* The precious facings and decorations of this mosque were removed by Maharaja Ranjit Singh to use the material elsewhere in his own buildings. Only a patch of tessellated marble flooring in the interior is still in place to testify to its past glory and later plunder when the Sikhs used this building as a stable for their horses.

19. Hindu Temple:

Originally the entrance to the *Shish Mahal* Complex (*Shah Burj*) towards west was through the south eastern side of the *Pa'een Bagh* Quadrangle. However, the Sikhs blocked this way by erecting an Hindu temple. It is on a raised platform in the shape of a cube crowned with a ribbed bulbous dome. The temple is dedicated to *Shiva* but otherwise it is a clumsy and unwarranted structure.

Hindu Temple.

G. *Shish Mahal Complex:*

The north-western part of the Fort consists of buildings basically having their origin in the days of the Emperor Shahjahan, though later additions of the Sikhs are also still found. This area has the signal distinction of portraying some of the real jewels in architecture and in building decorations of seventeenth century.

20. Forecourt of *Shish Mahal* :

The main access to the Forecourt of the Complex is through a large arched gateway, in the shape of an ornate vestibule. The interior of this is decorated with panels of frescoes. Although the courtyard is now provided with terraced flooring, there are sufficient indications of the presence of a small garden instead. Before the Sikhs vandalised the area, it had a big shallow tank with fountains in the centre, and symmetrically arranged walkways. On the eastern end there still exists a smaller version of *Sawan Bhadon,* on the pattern of that found in the Shalamar Garden, and a brick-built well not far away.

There was a pavilion in the middle of the northern fortification, and a marble screen railing possibly running over the whole length.

Entrance to the Shish Mahal Fore Court.

84

21. *Athdara:*

The north-west corner of the Square is now occupied by *Athdara,* an open pavilion having eight doorways. It dates back to the period of Maharaja Ranjit Singh who used it to hold his *katcheri* or court of justice.

The over-all impact of this building is not unpleasant, but it has a typical Sikh stamp if seen in detail. Some of such pitfalls are vivid in the combination of white marble with red sandstone brackets, marble trellis screens with red sandstone *mutaqqas* or posts in ornamental railing provided at the roof of the building, etc.

The northern wall of the *Athdara* has, quite unusually, some of the most pleasing specimens of fresco paintings. Set in panels, these frescoes depict scenes from the Hindu mythology and are distinguished to be of Sikh origin because of the gaudy colour scheme.

A view of Athdara in the forecourt of Shish Mahal.

22. *Samman Burj* or *Shah Burj:*

A high wall built by Maharaja Ranjit Singh now separates the forecourt from the Palace buildings of the *Samman Burj* on the western side. Both the courts must have been part of one complex, separated only by marble railing now crowning the *Athdara.* This fact has recently been confirmed during the conservation operations under the direction of the author. A small niche made under the high wall west of the *Shish Mahal* Complex showed the continuation of the floor with holes of the removed-posts towards eastern end.

The word *Samman* originally comes from the Arabic word *Musamman* meaning octagonal. The *Shish Mahal* interestingly is found built on a semi-octagonal plan. The original sources as also the inscription over the *Hathi Pol,* however, refer to these buildings in the context of completion as *Shah Burj* or the Royal Tower.

The construction of the *Samman Burj* goes back to the reigns of Jahangir and Shahjahan, its completion having been effected in 1631-32. The Sikhs also had their share of adding buildings to this complex, even if marring the original beauty through their ugly structures.

The exact usage of the buildings of the *Shah Burj* is not mentioned in any of the source records. It may be assumed that they belonged to the private apartments occupied by the Emperor and his *Harem.*

23. *Shish Mahal*:

The *Shah Burj* or the *Shish Mahal* is perhaps the most fabulous and most ornate part of the Royal Palace. It was created by the Emperor Shahjahan for

General View of Shish Mahal, also showing the shallow tank and water channels.

his beloved Empress Mumtaz Mahal, 'the lady of the Taj', called so as she lies buried in the *Taj Mahal* which now for long stands as one of the seven wonders of the world, also built by the same Emperor. Ironically she could not live in the *Shish Mahal* as she died in Aurangabad in 1631.

On plan the complex is a square having a series of *Dalans*, porticoes and pavilions arranged on all the sides of the courtyard. Four shallow water-channels divide the square courtyard into four parts. The channels are connected to a shallow tank in the midst of which is a *Mahtabi*, or a square platform, and four fountain-jets opposite each corner. The whole courtyard including the *Mahtabi* and the tank has been paved with variegated marble.

Shish Mahal: Complete View of the ceiling

Shish Mahal: View of the marble screen in back room.

Shish Mahal: Marble Screen.

There is a large hall, now known as *Shish Mahal* or the Palace of Mirrors, which occupies the north region of the square. Its longer side, facing the square, has a row of double five pillars. These pillars which are profusely decorated with delicately inlaid marble, form five archways surmounted by an eave of the same material. The spandrels over the arches and bases of the double columns of white marble are decorated with beautiful *pietra dura*. The main hall, rectangular in shape and having considerable dimensions, has a dado of white marble. The upper portion of the walls and the ceiling are embellished with extensive mosaic of glass laid in gypsum, which indeed has given it the most appropriate name of *Shish Mahal*, though the court chronicler Mullah Abdul Hamid Lahori mentions it just as *Aiwan* or Hall.

The glass decoration of the Hall clearly seems to belong to two periods. The ceiling with its prevailing aspect of subdued gilt and balanced style undoubtedly make it a part of the work done in the Mughal era. The wall

Shish Mahal's Large Hall.

decoration being gaudy and having the childish admixture of blue-and-white china must take its origin to the Sikhs.

The glass-work on the walls when fell off on peeling at a few places clearly showed the coarse paintings, also belonging to the Sikh period. Some of these paintings, still preserved, are based on the themes from the Hindu Mythology.

The roof of the 'Hall of Mirrors' is suspended from the wooden beams and rafters. Some of these beams showing decay were changed in the early part of twentieth century and then in the late 1980s. These conservation measures and the ageing process put together, have affected the binding strength of gypsum base further weakening the glass work at the ceiling.

Shish Mahal: A general view of ceiling and the wall of main Hall.

Shish Mahal's northern screen as seen from central arch.

The central hall is surrounded on three sides by a row of as many as nine rooms decorated in the same fashion. In the largest of these rooms, lying in the middle at the back of the main hall, there is a very fine marble *jali* or screen of trellis work.

The heavy and clumsy rooms, built by the Sikhs over the delicate *Shish Mahal* were in extremely dilapidated condition due to long period of neglect and disrepair. Some of these were removed to take off the dead weight, in the early years of the twentieth century during the *Raj*. The only remaining part over its eastern side, its building ascribed to Nau Nihal Singh, still mars the beauty of the *Shish Mahal.*

Delicate pietra-dura restored on bases of double-columns of Shish Mahal.

24. *Naulakha* Pavilion:

In the middle of the western extremity of the court lies an open pavilion commonly known as *Naulakha*. This name, as the tradition goes, refers to its having cost nine lakhs (900,000) of rupees. But the contemporary sources mention neither the name *Naulakha* nor the fabulous amount spent on its construction.

Built in the early years in the reign of the Emperor Shahjahan, this tiny but graceful pavilion is a simple oblong structure having a single arched opening in front, and a relatively smaller flat opening on each side. At the rear, this has a central archway flanked by smaller oblong openings filled with carved marble screens. The pavilion has a curvilinear roof, also known as Bangla style, placed over marble brackets.

The interior of the *Naulakha* has been lime-plastered, and in turn, treated with frescoes. The walls upto dado level are riveted with marble panels having inlay decorations. The pilasters, pillars, bases and other points have delicate and very fine *pietra dura* work.

Towards the north-eastern side of the open Court lies the apartment which is known as Sher Singh's Bathroom. It, however, dates back to the period of Shahjahan but was only altered by the Sikh Raja to suit his requirements of the *Hammam.*

A General View of Naulakha Pavilion.

94

Naulakha as viewed from Shish Mahal.

The court chronicler mentions of a set of seven apartments on the southern side of the square. Behind one of these used to be the Emperor's Sleeping Chamber (the *khwabgah),* decorated with marble dado and with views of the cities and gardens.

The *khwabgah* as such no longer existed even during the British period. It was perhaps the same *khwabgah* which around 1633 did not satisfy the refined taste of the Emperor Shahjahan and was replaced by the edifice now known as *chhoti khwabgah* which is located in the southern side of the Shahjahan's Quadrangle.

The central room has a chevron-patterned *aabshar,* or cascade, which was covered with plaster, probably during the Sikh period, but since uncovered. This portion of buildings was used as armoury by the Sikhs.

It is very fortunate that though some additions - notwithstanding their merits or demerits - were made by the Sikhs, generally speaking they did not mutilate or destroy at a scale usually witnessed in other buildings of the Mughal period. Their such a mellow behaviour must have been due to the fact that this complex remained a favourite abode with the Maharaja Ranjit Singh and his successors.

Panels with exquisite pietra-dura in Naulakha Pavilion

25. *Hathi Pol:*

The *Shah Burj or Saman Burj* was approached directly from outside the Fort. On the western side of the main entrance to the fore-court of the complex lies a large stairway called the *Hathi Pol or Hathi Paer/Hathi Paon* meaning the foot of elephant.

Built simultaneously with the *Shah Burj,* the three-flight stair consists of 58 low but broad steps connecting *Hathi Pol* Gate with the outer courtyard of the *Shish Mahal.* It was meant for the elephants of the royalty from and to the Palace.

The stairway is flanked by high panelled walls with imitation brick-work, *tazakari.* The western wall is provided, in both storeys, with niches where-in stood *Khwajasaras* (eunuchs), *Naqib* (announcers) and guards. The upper gallery known as *Ghulam Gardish,* meant for servants and attendants, was connected to the *Shish Mahal.*

26. *Hathi Pol* Gate:

On the southern end of the large stairs, after a turn through the large arch-way, lies the grand and lofty main entrance, created in the shape of double-storeyed vestibule embellished with panels of exquisite tile mosaic decoration.

Hathi Pol Gate

The gate which leads to the *Shah Burj* and the *Harem* portion of the Fort, was meant as a private entrance of the royalty. Before the Sikhs built the outer defence wall and then the British created a Postern Gate through it, the *Hathi Pol* Gate was the major access on the river front.

Over the arch of the Gate there is a Persian inscription on white marble. It is carved in eloquent *Nast'aliq* characters and records historical details, telling about the construction of the *Shah Burj*. It consists of six couplets (*shi'r*) and gives the date as A.H. 1041, the 4th year of accession (to throne by Shahjahan), which should correspond to 1632. It also mentions that the *Burj* (tower) was built under the superintendence of the architect Ma'mur Khan.

شاہِ جم جاہ سلیمان قدر کیوان بارگاہ   درصفا و رفعت و لطف و ہوا برجی چنیں

کرسپہر مہر بر ترو دہ رایاتِ جلال   ازحصارِ چرخ نمودہ است و نماید جبال

ثانی صاحبقراں شاہِ جہاں کہ عدل و جود   بندہ یکدل مریدِ معتقد عبدالکریم

نیستش نوشیرواں ماند و افریدوں ہمال   بعد اتمام عمارت یافت این تاریخ سال

شاہ برجی حکم کرد احداث کز فرطِ علو   دانما چوں دولتِ این بادشاہ جم سپاہ

ہست بیروں سمجو عرشِ اعظم از دہم خیال   این ہمایوں برجِ عالی با و زآفت بی زوال

۱۰۴۱ ھ

27. Pictured Wall:

The most striking feature of architectural decoration of the Lahore Fort is the use of tile-mosaic found on its west and north walls. This part of the Fort presents the buildings belonging to the two of the Great Mughals, Jahangir and Shahjahan, hence dating to the first half of the 17th century. The subject matter and the technique of this decoration also boldly suggest that like a number of other arts and crafts introduced by the Mughals, it seems to have come to the South Asian Subcontinent from Iran.

A study would easily tell that this kind of architectural decoration remained mainly confined to the plains of Punjab. Such wall decoration is unique to the fort although it is not uncommon to see some mosques and garden-gateways embellished with tile-mosaic. Among notable examples of such wall adornment in Lahore are the Wazir Khan's Mosque, Mosque of Dai Anga, *Chauburji* Gateway, *Gulabi Bagh* Gateway, etc. As most of the buildings with tile-mosaic decoration owe their origin to the reign of Emperor Shahjahan, it is usually ascribed to have been practised largely during his time.

The wall decoration in the Lahore fort exhibits not only traditional geometrical and foliated designs but also depicts figures of living beings. This is one aspect which makes it totally different from the art applied to mosques and other religious buildings.

The whole length of the north and west faces of the wall is about 460 metres while it is nearly 15 metres in height. The surface of the wall, approximately 7,000 square metres, is divided into sunk panels. Although the cruel treatment meted out to the decoration through long period of neglect is evident from the total or partial disappearance of much of the decoration yet the embellishment still left on the wall speaks high of the magnitude and the grandeur of the exclusive artistic work.

on a lesser scale. However, there are two panels placed one above the other, on each side, and encased by borders of scrolling work in which flowers take prominent place.

There are two cornices running throughout the length of the wall. The lower one is at a height of about 5.5 metres while the upper one takes its place near the top. Under each cornice runs a broad band of uniform geometrical design. In the upper band a six-point star with lines in dark blue and a yellow dot in the centre is repeated while in the lower band *Swastika* design in turquoise blue runs in repetitive shape. The upper cornice is surmounted by a solid parapet decorated with oft-repeated *Kangura*-designed border.

Starting from the *Hathi Pol* Gate in the western wall, it is noted that whole area was profusely covered with tile-mosaics. The decoration on the right hand has now completely disappeared while on the left side the damage is done

Tile mosaics

99

The arched recesses running along the whole length of the wall are of different width. The narrow recesses are found to be divided into two by horizontal bands of tile-work. A projecting miniature balcony-window decorates each of the lower recesses. The exact use of these orielled windows is not known but they certainly add to the grace and variety of the decorated surface. It is a pity that they have suffered a great deal and have survived in somewhat perfect shape only at few places. The panels between the recesses and the upper band have crudely-pierced loop-holes. Most probably it is the work of Sikhs, during their later period.

There are beautiful friezes of figured panels running between two rows of arched recesses placed at about half the height of the wall. Here are depicted elephants, horses, humped camels, men and birds. The spandrels over the large arches are superbly done, decorating them with winged figures in flowing garments.

Beneath the central arch on the north-west face of the *Shah Burj* is remarkably depicted a scene with four horsemen playing Polo or *Chaugan*. Another royal sport, camel fight, is shown set in oblong panels under the two

Northern and Western views of the Pictured Wall.

side arches. Among the other decorations found are the figures of angels, demon-head and a vivid depiction of clouds.

Large patches of the northern wall are now almost totally devoid of the colour decoration. From the available evidence it can safely be inferred that the whole length of this side of the wall was profusely decorated, just like that found on the west. The tile-mosaic work on this side too exhibits human beings and beasts in addition to geometrical designs.

The whole length of the northern wall is divided into four projecting towers or *Burjs*. They, in fact, stand at the peripheral limits of two different quadrangles of the Fort. The larger towers are placed at the two northern corners of the square called *Khil'at Khana*, while the other two relatively smaller *Burjs* occupy the corners of the Jahangir's quadrangle.

The tile-mosaic decoration on the northern wall has suffered a great deal as most of its area had been affected by water disposed from the Fort towards

101

Mosaic pictured wall of Old Fort.

river. Even today we find refuse and rain water coming from above constantly, affecting adversely the decoration and the stability of the brick-work.

Even a cursory look at the colossal work of decoration will reveal that the artisans must have struck out a new line to enliven their master-pieces with men and animals. The work of this magnitude must have called for services of innumerable *Kashikars* and the success of execution depended on individual genius and experience. While the floral and geometric designs bear a masterly stamp, perhaps because their being of very common subject, the figured panels depict a marked difference in artistic merit. Some of the panels show perfection of hand while there are others which have been done quite amateurishly.

28. Sikh Period Defence Wall:

During the Sikh period when the river Ravi had further receded to the north, away from the foot of the Fort, it became imperative for the rulers to add a defensive wall against the threat from outside. A heavy fortification wall was then constructed which started from the Fort bastion at the north eastern corner of the *Hazuri Bagh* to meet the Akbar period portion of the citadel at its east, girdling it on the north side, leaving a moat inbetween. The wall so built was provided with bastions at regular intervals, and machilation holes for musketry almost throughout its length.

102

29. Postern Gate:

In order to undermine the military utility of the Fort, and to provide easier access for vehicular traffic, the British changed some of the original features of the Fort by carving out, in 1853, a simple doorway, the postern, through the Sikh period fortification wall at the western side.They also built, in 1899, a metalled road from the Postern Gate through Hathi Pol upto the *Diwan-e-Aam Quadrangle* by cutting through the higher ground of the Mughal area of buildings.

Postern Gate

30. Alamgiri Gate:

In the western high-crenellated wall of the Fort, opening on to the *Hazuri Bagh* is a highly imposing gate-way, called the Alamgiri Gate. The massive vestibule is surmounted by two elegant towers on either side. A curiously twisted passage led upto the western entrance of the *Diwan-e-Aam* Quadrangle.

A gate in this side of the wall is said to have been built by the Emperor Akbar. This is why some of the historians and writers tend to call it Akbari Gate, which however, is a misnomer. The present gate is in complete harmony with the massive and masculine construction of the main Entrance to the *Badshahi* Mosque. It was placed here by Aurnagzeb Alamgir at the time of the building of the latter mentioned edifice.

The Gate has witnessed many eventful scenes of history. It played important role in the successive strifes of the Sikhs for the 'throne' of Lahore. During the British period it was bricked up and closed for fear of the fort's military use against the *Raj.* It remained in that condition for more than two years even after achieving independence in 1947. On 18 November, 1949, it was re-opened by the Punjab Governor, Sardar Abdul Rab Nishtar, in an impressive ceremony when he termed it as the opening of a new chapter in the history of the Muslims.

The lofty portal now serves as the main entrance to the Fort and houses the Booking Office and some souvenir shops.

Alamgiri Gate with Sikh Baradari showing at right.

Hazuri Bagh with Badshahi Mosque Steps, Sikh Baradari, and Alamgiri Gate.

Hazuri Bagh with Sikh Baradari, outer Roshnai Gate and Ranjit Singh's Smadh.

Alamgiri Gate as viewed from an arch of Sikh Baradari.

BADSHAHI MASJID

The grand mosque, commonly known as the *Badshahi Masjid* or Regal Mosque, the last of the sumptuous accomplishments of the great Mughals, has remained a synonym with Lahore during the past over three hundred years. Situated west of the famous Lahore Fort, across the *Hazuri Bagh,* its lofty minarets can be seen from quite a distance around. Predominantly a red sandstone monument, the mosque indeed is a pleasant blend of strength, harmony and grace at their best. The exquisite *pietra dura* work and intricate fresco paintings in the interior present a charming beauty fused with sturdy merlons on wall giving it a martial look.

The main entrance to the mosque lies on the eastern side, opposite Alamgiri Gate of the Fort. A monument in itself, the gateway consists of a double-storey building with a three-centred central vault. An inscription on white marble tablet fixed over it, records in Persian the date of the completion of the mosque. Besides *Kalima,* the inscription tells that the mosque was built in 1673 (A.H.1084) for the Emperor Aurangzeb by Fidai Khan Koka.

مَسجد ابوالظفر محی الدّین محمد عالمگیر بادشاہ غازی سنہ ہزار و ہشتاد و چہار ہجری اتمام یافت

با اہتمام کمترین خانہ زادان فند ائیخان کوکہ

Badshahi Mosque: General view of main prayer chamber.

The mosque is built on a raised platform set on arches. It is square in plan and covers an area of 172 square metres. Each of the corners has a tall, stately *minar* in red sandstone, rising to a height of about 54 metres. The *Minars* are circular inside, each with vertical shaft set in the centre. A spiral staircase with 204 steps rise to the top pavilion which is surmounted by a white marble cupola.

The imposing entrance of the mosque is approached by a flight of 22 steps rising from three sides to reach a red sandstone platform. The entrance building presents a vivid example of traditional Mughal architecture at its peak. The façades are decorated with framed and carved panelling while square minarets surmounted by red sandstone pavilions and white marble cupolas on four corners add a unique grace to the stately look of the building.

Badshahi Mosque: A closer view of central arch.

The gateway opens on to a vast courtyard. It is enclosed with *Hujras* or cells all around excepting the portion in the west where the main prayer chamber is located. The courtyard is divided into upper and lower parts. The eastern portion, consisting of the lower part, accommodates the ablution tank which no more serves its original purpose. After renovations it has been beautified with white marble screen and a fountain which provides a soothing treat to the eye. For the purpose of ablution of the *namazis* or the prayer offerers the eastern cells, pulled down by the colonial masters in 1865, have been reconstructed to serve as long ablution halls, in addition to housing a Quran Gallery in the northern wing. The courtyard was originally built in small cut country bricks. During the renovations this badly decayed floor was replaced with sandstone slabs.

The upper part of the courtyard is just a step higher. The gigantic building of the Prayer Chamber lies in its western portion. The building is set

Badshahi Mosque: Interior view of the prayer chamber.

Badshahi Mosque: A closer look at domes and some minarets.

on a raised platform reached by flight of steps in *Sang-e-Abri*. The eastern façade has three-centred central vault flanked by five smaller arches on either side. The red sandstone facing is provided with well-proportioned panelling decorated with marble inlay in lineal, floral and geometrical patterns. The beautiful design in bold relief depicting intertwining of blooming flowers with their spidery tendrils, called *zanjira*, is the masterpiece of craftsmanship. The interior is decorated with floral patterns in relief on lime-plastered surface, and tastefully done fresco paintings in bright colours.

The main structure consists of two deep and long halls. The front one is divided into two halls, one on each side of the central vault. The back portion comprises of seven bays connected through eight heavy arches on massive jambs. The floor which was originally built in cut country bricks has been replaced by white marble, patterned as *Musallahs* lined with *Sang-e-Abri*.

On top, three bulbous domes in white marble dominate the sky-line with four corner-minarets surmounted by pavilions having white marble cupolas with gilded pinnacles of copper. All these features put together produce an enchanting effect of harmony and beauty par excellence.

The mosque has seen many ups and downs in its history. In addition to a big jolt in an earthquake in 1840, the Sikh rulers also damaged it considerably. During the reign of Ranjit Singh the mosque building was used as a magazine for military stores. The ensuing Sikh wars of succession saw it being used repeatedly for military purpose. The matchlock men of Sher Singh occupied the *Minars* when he besieged the nearby Fort in 1841. Not long after, light guns mounted on them bombarded the Fort, resulting in the destruction

Badshahi Mosque: Lit at night.

113

Badshahi Mosque: Main Entrance, in itself a monument.

of many buildings including Shahjahan's *Diwan-e-Aam,* as Hira Singh was forcing out the besieged Sindhanwala *Sirdars.*

The mosque remained in the possession of Sikhs till the annexation of Punjab by the British in 1849. The British also used it as powder magazine but carried out some of the first repairs in 1850. To defray the repair costs, the British authorities chose to sell its red sandstone slabs. It was, however, strongly resented by the Muslim population and as a result, further sale was stopped. The mosque was restored to Muslims in 1856 only after dismantling the eastern cells to prevent its use as a stronghold against the British.

At the time of its restoration to Muslims, the mosque was in a shattered condition. Major repairs were undertaken intermittently to consolidate the structure and rebuild the decayed or missing portions. These repairs, however, did not take into consideration the guidelines set for scientific conservation of ancient monuments hence difference in material used and change in some of the original features.

It is indeed heartening that the conservation work recently carried out was mainly on scientific lines, to restore the original features of the mosque. The red sandstone, stripped off from the facing of the cells during Sikh and British periods, has been re-applied systematically with the stone especially imported from India, to match the original material. With these restoration operations the *Shahi Masjid* has once again gained much of its original shape.

Badshahi Mosque: Lit at night.

Shalamar Garden: View of the second and third terraces, from central Baradari.

SHALAMAR GARDENS

Towards east of Lahore lies the Shalamar Garden which is one of the best specimens of the art of land-scaping introduced by the Mughals in the South Asian Subcontinent. It is in the form of an oblong parallelogram surrounded by a high brick-wall. The garden comprises of three successive terraces, raised one above the level of the other.

Emperor Shahjahan had proved his abilities as an outstanding architect and horticulturist even before he ascended the throne in 1627. The first master-piece of the Shalamar series of gardens was laid by him under the command of his father Emperor Jahangir, in 1618-19 at Srinagar, Kashmir. The natural terraced terrain of the hilly place was indeed a boon for the refined aesthete like Shahjahan. About quarter of a century later he must have faced the drawback for a similar exercise in a monotonously flat plain of Punjab. Thanks to the inherent skill and ingenuity of this gifted man that he overcame the difficulty and created a real terraced garden. It became popular by the same name, Shalamar, although the Emperor himself would call the upper terrace as *Farah Bakhsh* or Pleasure-giving, and the middle and lower terraces together as *Faiz Bakhsh* or bounty-giving.

The garden was completed at a cost of six lacs of rupees (Rs. 600,000) on July 12, 1641, in one year, five months and four days under the superintendence of Khalil ullah Khan.

There are a number of interpretations and explanations for the name Shalamar but plausible meanings have yet to be assigned to its attachment

Shalamar Garden: Central Tank and the Red Sandstone Baradari.

with these gardens. This name has been on record since as far back as 1654 when Muhammad Salih Kamboh compiled his *Bahar-e-Sukhan.* This only goes to prove that it had already been started being called a Shalamar in the popular jargon when the royal name of *Farah Bakhsh* and *Faiz Bakhsh* were used by the Emperor.

In the absence of any earlier instance, the idea of a garden in terraces with enclosure walls, a number of pavilions, and canals running through the centre, is attributed to the Mughals as an innovation in the Sub-continent. The rows of fountains running throughout the length of the central and intersecting canals, and symmetrically arranged in the tanks only add beauty to the scene.

The garden spreads over a total area of about 17 hectares of which about 2/3rd is devoted to plantation while canals, tanks and pavilions cover the rest of the land. The length of the central and intersecting canals running over the first terrace i.e. *Farah Bakhsh* is 455 metres while in the third terrace it measures 461 metres.

One hundred and five fountains play in the first terrace, 152 in the second and 153 in the lowermost terrace bringing the total count to four hundred and ten. In addition to these hydraulic features there are five cascades and the famous *Sawan Bhadon,* and *Hammam* or royal baths with running hot and cold water. These are in addition to the provision to irrigate the greenery of the Shalamar.

Shalamar Garden: Aabshar or cascade coming down from Ist terrace.

118

Upper Terrace:

The uppermost or the first terrace in the present arrangements, called *Farah Bakhsh*, is square on plan. It is modelled perfectly on Persian *charbagh* style. It comprises eight buildings, four in the middle of sides and four in the corners. The *Khwabgah* or the sleeping chamber of the Emperor was created on the south while that of the Empress on the west along the perimeter wall. Both of these buildings are elaborate double-storeyed pavilions having side rooms and a relatively larger central room, decorated with marble inlay, gilded stucco and tracery, and fresco paintings. The Emperor's Sleeping Chamber has a beautiful shallow bowl shaped marble cistern with a fountain in the centre.

A similar cistern, but of jade, was also provided in the Empress' *Khwabgah*. The *Aramgah*, as the *Khwabgah* of the Emperor is also known, was re-modified during the British period by opening a gate on the south, to provide access to the Garden from the then newly laid Grand Trunk Road.

The building in the middle of the northern side of the terrace is a vast pavilion which was a resting place of the Emperor, known as *Tambikhana*. It originally had brick-vaulting, marble dado and marble inlaid floor. Much of its such features were changed by the Sikhs, as they removed most of the stone while also changed the roof with the one having typically gaudy *tarseemkari*.

Shalamar Garden: A view of the Ist Terrace's Central Baradari and 2nd terrace's Tank from Red Sand stone pavilion.

119

Middle Terrace:

The central or the middle terrace is more elaborate for buildings, as also for the hydraulic arrangements. Oblong on plan, it is the first stage of *Faiz Bakhsh* and in it has pavilions, *hammam,* a very large tank with matching *Mahtabi* in the centre, *Sawan Bhadon,* marble throne, an *Aabshar* or cascade and elaborate rose garden. The central portion of the terrace, containing the tank and the pavilions, is higher than its flanks, on east and west, which are occupied by the rose garden.

Royal Hammam:

A very elaborate *Hammam* or Royal Bath lies in the eastern perimeter wall of the second terrace, near the south-eastern corner. Although projecting outwards, it is not distinctly recognisable from outside as it shares its façade with that of the eastern wall of the garden. The *Hammam* itself is a single-

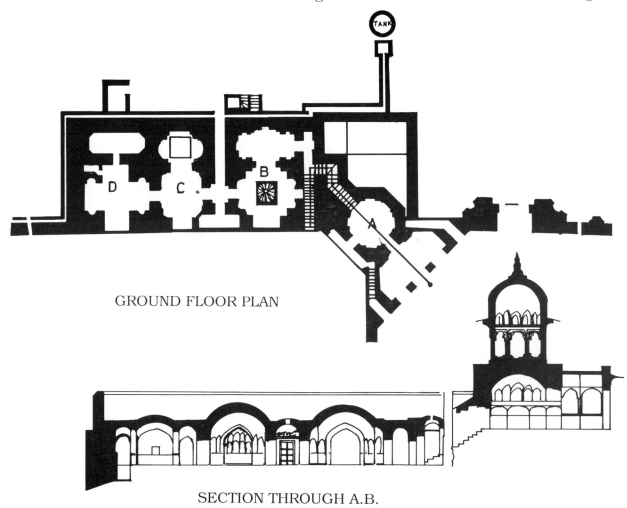

GROUND FLOOR PLAN

SECTION THROUGH A.B.

HAMMAM INSIDE
SHALAMAR GARDEN AT LAHORE

SCALE:- 3 0 3 6 9 METRES

storeyed structure, modest in height to preserve heat. It is designed on the longitudinal axis and approached by two entrances - one each from the first and the second terraces.

The access from the first terrace or *Farah Bakhsh*, the quarters for the use of royalty, is through a semi-octagonal alcove, ending up into octagonal chamber with a balcony projecting over the middle terrace. This room is surmounted by a pavilion and approached by a flight of steps on either side of the alcove. The octagonal chamber of the first terrace leads through a flight of steps into a narrow passage lying in an east-west direction opening up into the middle terrace. There are two door-ways leading from it to the first apartment of the *Hammam*.

The *Hammam* consists of three main apartments running from south to north. The first room was the *Rakht Khana* - the place for dressing - or *Jama Khana* where clothes are removed. It is divided into two parts. The western portion, cruciform in shape, contains a square fountain basin in the

Shalamar Garden: 2nd Terrace: Central Tank and Red Sandstone Pavilion.
A part of Sawan Bhadon is seen in the foreground.

121

centre. It was meant for refreshments before and after the bath. The eastern part, rectangular in shape having an independent opening from the passage served as the dressing room. The *Rakht Khana* is separated from the next room by a vaulted space which opens out of the garden, though it stands blocked now. On western extremity of this passage is a narrow room which was used for the management and cleaning of the *Hammam.*

The next which is the central room, also consists on two parts. The western part is a square chamber with chamfered inner angles and arched recesses on eastern and western sides. The eastern octagonal part with an arched recess in the eastern wall, has a square water tank in the middle. The tank could be used for cold or hot baths, as desired.

A rectangular opening leads from here to the last apartment of the *Hammam.* Cruciform in shape, the quarter has a rectangular water tank in its northern arm. There is a marble jet in the shape of a lion-head at each corner of the tank except one which is on the south-eastern side. This apartment contains two water-reservoirs of which the eastern, and by fart the larger, reservoir is in oblong octagonal shape, having two terra-cotta pipes. There is a round opening in the floor, covered by a metallic sheet to ensure maximum heat from the furnace under the floor. The other reservoir in the thickness of the wall, is of small dimensions and meant for storage of cold water.

Shalamar Garden: A General View of the Second Terrace.

Lower Terrace:

The lowermost terrace or the second stage of the *Faiz Bakhsh* had no elaborate buildings except a pavilion in the middle of the northern wall, where the central canal ends to discharge its water in the outer garden. The only two elaborately designed gateways, one each in the eastern and the western perimeter walls, were provided in this terrace. The entourage entered from these gates and camped in the *Faiz Bakhsh*, the lower two terraces, while the upper terrace, *Farah Bakhsh*, was reserved for the exclusive use of the Emperor with the royal *Harem*.

Shalamar Garden: Central Tank and Baradari
as seen from northern pavilion.

THE HYDRAULICS OF SHALAMAR

It may be remarked that the very first thing noticeable in Mughal architectural planning or landscaping is their fondness for flowing water. Be it a sleeping chamber, a hall of private or public audience, a pleasure or a formal garden - or even a memorial for a dead monarch - The focal object would invariably be water. Their love for flowing water sometimes reaches an obsession. It reminds one of their ancestral homeland in the arid climate of Central Asia where flowing water is a dream of luxury.

The historians of art have devoted a great deal of efforts in extolling the masonry art of Mughal architecture, but very little has been said about their skill in hydraulic engineering. The contemporary records tell only of the irrigating system or, at the most, give a plain description of fountains and cascades. No details are found of the system adopted to tame and channelize water to run the canals, cascades and, above all, fountains to get the desired effect.

The feat of hydraulic engineering devised by the great Mughal for the Shalamar Garden is complicated but nevertheless very interesting. As the natural physiography of the plains did not provide an adequate quantity of water with desired hydraulic pressure, lacking any springs and the natural gradient, the foremost priority was that of devising means to overcome this difficulty. First of all a spot with just enough slope was selected on the left bank of river Ravi before it reached Lahore. To have constant and somewhat natural flow of water, and finally disposal of its remaining part posed other problems. The first great task undertaken to meet the challenge was to branch off a canal from the river Ravi at Madhupur, about 160 kilometres upstream where the river emerges from mountains to the plains.

The canal which came to be known as *Shah Nahr* or the Royal Canal was designed by Ali Mardan Khan in such a way as to arrange flow of water upto the southern portion of the Shalamar, considerably higher than the river running on its north. The project, indeed a marvel in itself, cost rupees 150,000 but did not work well. The job was then assigned to Mulla Ala al-Mulk Tuni who, after spending another 50,000 rupees was able to achieve the desired results. The *Shah Nahr* was now flowing full with water from Madhupur to Lahore considerably higher than the corresponding level of the Ravi running almost parallel to it. The canal later on came to be known as *Hansli* Canal and finally the Shalamar Distributory till its closure in 1958 as a result of non-availability of water in pursuance of the Indus Water Treaty with India.

The water of *Shah Nahr* was used for two purposes: a) irrigation of the complex of gardens including Shalamar, and b) filling of the canals of the upper terrace and the main tank in the middle terrace.

In the absence of any blue prints or plans of the hydraulic layout of the Shalamar it had remained quite a puzzle for even the modern engineers. During the late 1970s and early 80s a host of conservation problems of the Shalamar Garden proved 'blessing in disguise' at least in the better understanding of the system which supplied water at a desired pressure to 410 fountains, enabled five cascades to run with even flow, allowed all the canals and tanks to remain full to the brim yet not permitting a single drop to spill over the beautiful brick-on-edge pavement, and made the *Sawan Bhadon* play constantly the sweet *musique de l'eau*.

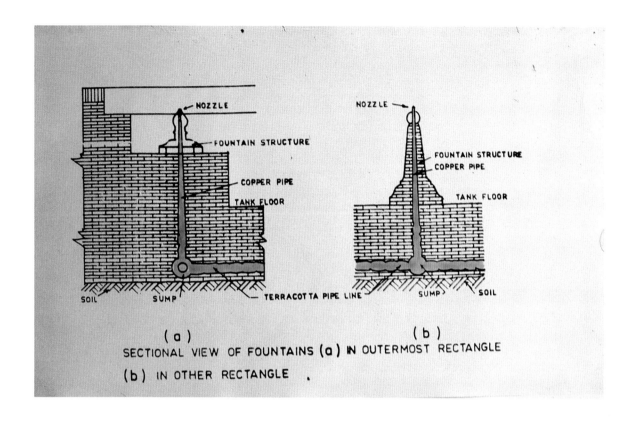

SECTIONAL VIEW OF FOUNTAINS (a) IN OUTERMOST RECTANGLE
(b) IN OTHER RECTANGLE .

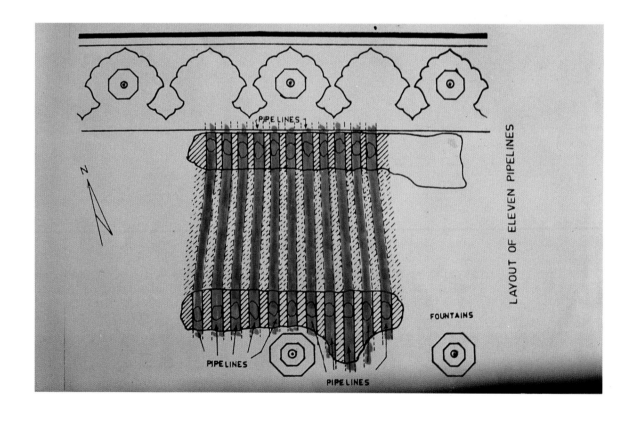

LAYOUT OF ELEVEN PIPELINES

The *Shah Nahr* water was mainly used to irrigate gardens in addition to the filling of the first terrace canals. The Royal canal perhaps could not maintain the constant flow of water throughout the year. Moreover, it might not have been found feasible to lift this clay-laden water to develop pressure for playing the fountains. It was, therefore, necessary to exploit other water sources for silt-free supply to avoid the possibility of choking the outlets and underground pipes. This additional water supply was provided from a complex on the southern side of the Shalamar. A well, with Persian wheel, ensured the constant supply of clear water. An over-head reservoir was constructed at a height of about 8 metres from the bed level of the first terrace's central canal. The reservoir consisted of two inter-connected tanks. The water lifted from the well was discharged into the main tank measuring 19m x 5.5m. Three holes, each with 10cm diameter, transferred the water to the next tank of 5.5m x 3.3m dimensions. The latter served as the filtration tank where sand particles in water would settle down. The water then travelled to two chambers, 3.5m x 2.2m and 2.2m x 1.3m size, through four holes positioned vertically. The depth of all the tanks including chambers was kept uniform at 1.4m.

The reservoirs are built in solid brick masonry and outlets, where provided, have been chiselled out in one-piece red sandstone blocks. From the western side of the large chamber a 15cm diameter outlet provided water to the pipe which was downed and kept underground while another such outlet was also placed in the eastern chamber of lesser dimensions. Although it is now difficult to lay exploratory trenches to ascertain the exact location of the pipeline under the ground yet its entry into the upper terrace from under the *Aramgah* (now serving as main access) has helped reconstruct its path already mentioned by the historians. The terracotta pipe with a diameter of 18cm lay embedded 1.8m below the level of the bed of the canal.

The terracotta pipe was almost always hand-moulded, each length varying from 30cm to 35cm. In order to join them together, one end of each pipe-piece was made collared, 1.2cm larger in diameter.

The simple fitting of one piece into the other would certainly not have served purpose of water supply without loss of much of water thereby affecting the over-all pressure as well as damaging the structures through seepage. The methods devised for sealing off the joints for the purpose of better water supply and even pressure throughout the length of the pipline, were so perfect that it has served the purpose for over three hundred and fifty years.

Hessian was wrapped on the free-end of the pipeline. It was then fixed into the collared end. The cavities still left were filled by pushing jute threads. The evidence shows that hessian was dipped in white lime cream which was waxy in feeling. The laboratory analysis of the material has not yet been able to identify the greasy component though it is presumed that it was used to enhance the impermeability of the cloth. To seal off the whole joint for complete reassurance of its being leak-proof, it was plastered with fine *kankar* lime mixed with white lime. The terracotta pipeline was then lime-plastered and embedded in solid masonry work to increase its life.

The hydraulic system of the Shalamar Garden is so perfectly planned that one only wonders at the skill and vision of its creators. In addition to the arrangements and placement of pipelines, the technique evolved for the running of fountains and giving a long choke-free life to the underground water

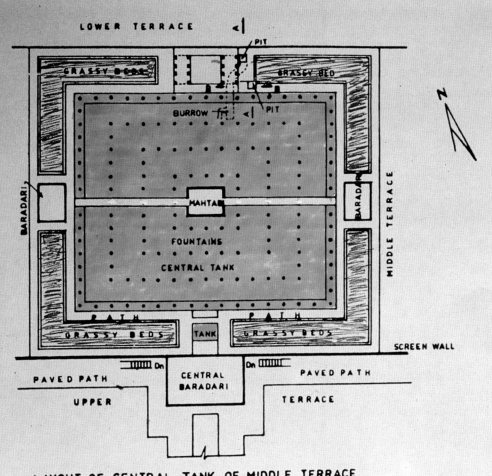

LAYOUT OF CENTRAL TANK OF MIDDLE TERRACE

0 4 8 12 16 20 metres

Scale.

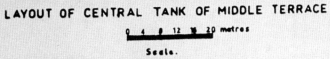

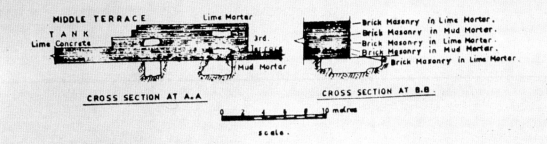

MIDDLE TERRACE

TANK

Lime Concrete

Lime Mortar

3rd

Mud Mortar

CROSS SECTION AT A.A

Brick Masonry in Lime Mortar.
Brick Masonry in Mud Mortar.
Brick Masonry in Lime Mortar.
Brick Masonry in Mud Mortar.
Brick Masonry in Lime Mortar.

CROSS SECTION AT B.B.

0 2 4 6 8 10 metres

scale.

supply system in itself is not less than a marvel. As has already been mentioned, the terracotta pipeline ran at a depth of 1.8m under the canal bed. At every fountain point a vertical near-oval-shaped sump was provided in line with the supply pipe, in a thick and solid masonry. The pipeline was connected to the sump on both sides serving as inlet and outlet, about half way up its bottom. This arrangement always left enough water stored here to keep the uniformity of water pressure in the fountains. The underground chamber of each fountain would also have served as a filtration space, always leaving the pipeline clean and clear. On the top of the said chamber a horizontally projected copper plate, usually 3mm in thickness, was fixed and plastered tight to the main body of the reservoir. A hole was provided in the centre of the plate where another terracotta pipe of 7.7cm diameter was fixed.

The baked pipe, in turn, was replaced by a tapered one, this time made of copper sheet, with the upper orifice usually of 2cm diameter. The metal pipe was simply made by overlapping the ends of a sheet and was fixed in the thick brick-masonry work provided on top with a carved one-piece red sandstone block which served as fountain head. The water came out gushing from the copper pipe which does not seem to have been provided with any shoots of the modern concept of garden fountain. There remained enough pressure to raise the fountain water to a height ranging from 3.5m to 3.75m.

The main pipeline of 15.3 cm diameter, coming from the complex on southern side of the garden was certainly incapable of supplying the required quantity of water throughout the garden. To augment the deficiency, the eastern outlet from the main overhead reservoir was used. An outlet, similar in design and size to that on the western side, was connected to a terracotta pipe which was laid underground upto the eastern perimeter wall. It runs on the wall and is downed at a spot near *Naqqarkhanah* where it is connected with 1.8m deep main supply pipe at its eastern end.

Another such connection has been made available from the western side. On the outer fringe of the western perimeter wall, not far from the end of the canal, water was lifted to the overhead tank from where a pipeline, downed from the wall, connected at the western end of the main supply line running under the row of the fountains.

For the supply of sufficient water to the fountains of the upper terrace the above mentioned two connections in addition to the main supply from southern side, worked with satisfaction for the designers. However, the supply of the water to maintain desired pressure in the fountains of the lower-most terrace perhaps made the job somewhat difficult. To feed these fountains two more connections, one on each end of the east-west canal, were given. The western connection took its supply, through an *aqueduct* along the western perimeter wall, from the overhead reservoir situated west of the uppermost terrace, from where the water supply to the first terrace was also augmented. A well, located near the north-eastern *Burj* of the first terrace, supplied water to the eastern end via the overhead reservoir and *aqueduct* running on the perimeter wall.

Coming back to the upper terrace we find that the water supplied from the *Shah Nahr* multiplied by that discharged into the canal by playing of 105 fountains would not hold itself within limits unless channelized properly with precise calculations. The hydraulic engineering achieved another feat by

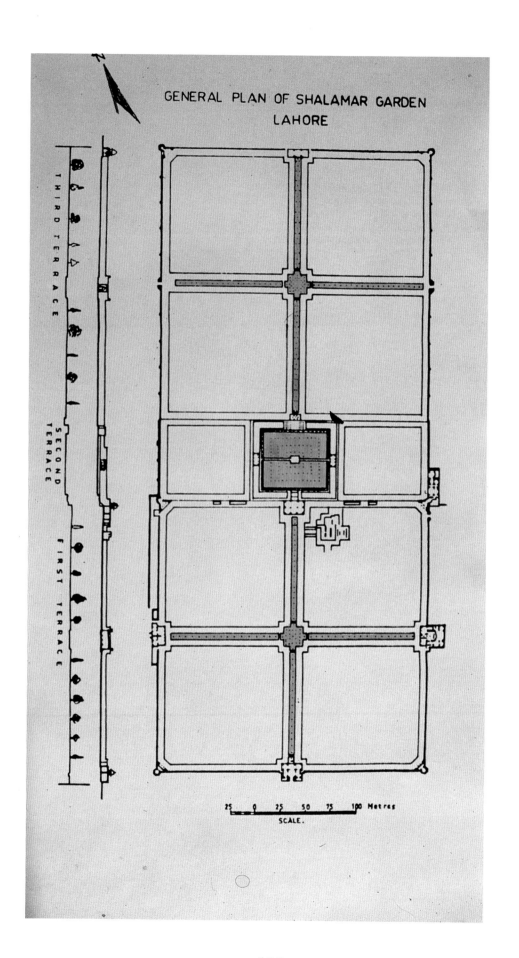

GENERAL PLAN OF SHALAMAR GARDEN
LAHORE

THIRD TERRACE

SECOND
TERRACE

FIRST TERRACE

25 0 25 50 75 100 Metres
SCALE.

utilising this surplus water for the running of the main marble cascade and 152 fountains of the middle terrace.

At the end of the central canal, just near the pavilion, eight feeding points in the form of inlet pipes, four from each side of the channel, were provided for fountains of the main tank of the middle terrace, *Sawan Bhadon* and eventually for running of the fountains of the third terrace. The extraordinary thickness of the solid brick masonry has always proved a barrier against ascertaining the exact layout of these pipelines. There positioning, however, suggests that they pass under, or close to the central *Baradari.*

Similar difficulties are faced with the central tank of the middle terrace where 152 fountains are arranged in 4 rectangles in an impressive symmetry. The floor of the tank has been laid in about two-metre thick solid brick masonry in lime mortar. It, once again, rendered it impossible to know the exact routes of the pipelines laid under the thick and heavy floor. Faced with this difficulty especially during a leakage, archaeologists and conservationists had to seek the help of nuclear scientists to locate the pattern of the pipeline grid. The sealed radiation source method cleared the picture to some extent. Now we know for sure that all the fountains of the central tank were inter-connected. It was, indeed, also necessary to produce harmony in their proper playing.

This tank served as the main reservoir to supply water to *Sawan Bhadon* and to the fountains of the lower-most terrace. After filling the tank, the water

split into two small cascades, on east and west sides, and flowing over the *Sawan Bhadon,* discharged into the canals of the lower terrace. A part of the water in the central tank was channelized through pipeline to feed the fountains of the third terrace. Eleven pipes served as feeding points for the purpose. The arrangement of these lines was made on a sophisticated and precise plan to make the maximum use of the water in the tank. Three pipelines were used to feed three parallel rows of fountains in the central canal of the third terrace: four pipes fed the five fountains located in the inner basin of *Sawan Bhadon* while the remaining four pipelines supplied water to two cascades of the *Chini Khana.*

The water from the cascades and fountains filled the canal of the third terrace. Its disposal was finally arranged through drains under the *Baradari* at the northern-most end of the central canal. Outside the perimeter wall of the garden, this water was used to irrigate *Mahtabi Bagh,* a fruit garden, and a large tank situated in it. The surplus water was drained out to the river Ravi flowing at the extreme north side.

Wazir Khan's Mosque: The Mehrab or the niche.

MASJID WAZIR KHAN

While entering the old, walled city of Lahore through the Delhi Gate, one finds a narrow bazaar flanked by an assortment of shops and houses. The bazaar is further narrowed by hand-carts, tongas, bicycles and occasional automobile transporting merchandise, commuting shoppers or residents. The people still walk casually, are seen engrossed in gossip quite oblivious of the surroundings. You experience the honking of all sorts of sound signals and yelling for the way through this mess of men and their machines.

The scene takes you back in time and, even if temporarily, you feel transported into the past of the city. Indeed a few more minutes walk would find you standing face to face with the past typified in the shape of a beautiful edifice, known as Wazir Khan's *Masjid*, or the Mosque of Wazir Khan which once was the centre of religious and educational activities of the thriving city.

The mosque stands at the site of the tomb of Sayyid Muhammad Ishaq, alias Miran Badshah, who came from Iran and settled in Lahore during the Tughlaq period. The tomb, now within the premises of the mosque, is still the centre of veneration for many a devotee of the saintly personage. The mosque, however, gets the name from its builder better known by his title, Wazir Khan.

Wazir Khan's Mosque: Façade of the prayer chamber
with ablution tank in the foreground.

Wazir Khan's Mosque: The Minret.

His real name was Ilm-ud-din Ansari son of Sheikh Abdul Latif who hailed from Chiniot, a prosperous town by the bank of the river Chenab in Punjab. Mullah Abdul Hameed Lahori, a contemporary historian and author of *Badshahnama*, tells that after acquiring the knowledge of Arabic and Philosophy, Ilm-ud-din became a student of *Hakim* (Physician) Dawai from whom he learned medicine to practise as profession.

As a *Hakim* (physician) he entered the service of Prince Khurram who was later to become the Emperor Shahjahan. His achievement as physician attracted the eye of the Prince who appointed him as *Diwan* (superintendent of House-hold). Later, he was made *Mir Saman* or the superintendent of the Royal Kitchen.

The Prince was so much pleased with the devotion to duty of the *Hakim* that after ascending to the throne in 1628 he raised him to the command of 7,000 and bestowed on him the title of Wazir Khan. He was subsequently elevated to the coveted position of the Governor of Punjab in which capacity he served the Emperor for seven years, from 1632 to 1639.

Wazir Khan, like his Emperor, had a good sense of planning buildings and an appreciative eye for the decorative art practised on them. In addition to the said mosque he constructed buildings like *Hammams, serais* and *Baradaris* or pavilions.

The grace and elegance in architectural style and surpassing beauty in decoration make the Wazir Khan's *Masjid* stand out prominently amongst the prized buildings of the Mughal period. It is a rare example of profused decoration of variegated glazed tiles, colourful paintings, impeccable *tazakari* or brick-imitation work, and superb calligraphy. It is almost completely covered with arabesque paintings and multi-coloured tiles, using eight colours to be precise. The pieces of glazed tiles are set so immaculately as to give the impression of paintings depicting flowers, leaves, trees and vases. The fancy decoration in painting on the walls presents the true fresco work known as *Buono* type fresco in which paintings are set when the plaster is still loose so the pigments mixed with water or water-and-lime go deep into the skin and cannot be removed when dry unless the whole of the plaster is removed.

The mosque is built on a raised platform with a flight of steps leading to the beautiful entrance on the east. The façade of the arched entrance is profusely decorated with floral designs and calligraphy executed masterfully. The domed entrance, an edifice in itself, opens into a vast courtyard in the middle of which lies the traditional clear-water tank for the ablution of the *Faithfuls*. At each corner of the quadrangle is a minaret rising to a stately height, provided with spiral staircase inside. These minarets excel in grandeur and beauty of decoration. The only other example to match such an extra-ordinary craftsmanship is found in the *minars* of Jahangir's Tomb, also an achievement of the same period.

The main building of the mosque lying on the customary western side of the courtyard is divided into five compartments, each one surmounted by a dome and opening on to the courtyard through an arched doorway. The central arch and dome rise higher than the flanking two arches and the domes on either side.

The rows of *Hujras* (cells) provided in the enclosure wall are said to have served for practising different artistic trades as well as housing a *madrassa*.

محمد عربی کا بروی هر دو سرا است،
کسی که خاک درش نیست چاک برساد

سال تاریخ بنائے مسجد عالی مقام در عهد ابو المظفر صاحبقران ثانی
از فرد چشم بگفتا سجده گاه اهل فضل شاہ جہاں بادشاہ غازی اتمام یافت
تا ریخ این بنای چوں پرسیدم از خرد بانی بیت اللہ ثانی فردوی باخلاص
گفت بگو که بانی مسجد وزیر خان مرید خاص الخاص قدیم الخدمت وزیر خان

Two Persian chronograms inscribed on the front gateway give the date of founding of the mosque as A.H. 1044 which corresponds to 1634. In 1641 Wazir Khan created a Trust by writing a *Waqf* Deed for the support of the mosque and its establishment. Through this instrument he bequeathed permanently his property consisting of all the shops and houses on either side of the street from the mosque to Delhi Gate, together with the *Serai and Hammams* close to Delhi Gate.

In spite of the fore-sightedness of Wazir Khan to provide a continuous support for the maintenance and upkeep of the mosque, the vagaries of time did

Wazir Khan's Mosque: A Geometrical-cum-floral pattern.

136

not show any mercy on the building unsurpassed in majestic architecture and exquisite embellishment. The tastefully done tile mosaic decoration and the true fresco paintings had decayed considerably at the turn of the nineteenth century, almost 250 years after its construction. It was mainly because of the fact that the trades and arts practised here had fallen into neglect due to lack of patronage on the part of the rulers after the Mughals. An aesthete and scholar like J.L.Kipling, one time Principal of the famous Mayo School of Arts, laments its condition as he found it in 1890. But it was not before the early seventies of the twentieth century that due attention was paid towards its conservation and restoration.

It indeed took a lot of hard work, patience and high degree of commitment to restore the half-perished arts in tile-mosaic and fresco paintings. The few artisans available from the lineage of the old masters were encouraged and still more craftsmen inducted into the profession and trained to undrtake and complete the glory of this unique specimen of artistic accomplishment. The dedication and zeal of the experts and the workmen have borne very rewarding fruit. Most of its lost splendour has now been regained to enchant the beholder and to give the edifice a fresh lease of life.

Wazir Khan's Mosque: A floral pattern in mosaic.

WAZIR KHAN'S BARADARI

After Hakim Ilm-ud-din alias Nawab Wazir Khan had finished the building of the mosque known after his name, he turned his attention to laying of a vast garden in the neighbourhood of the city of Lahore. The garden came to be known as *Nakhlia* because of its containing a large number of date trees. The garden was adorned with a building of *Baradari,* or the pavilion with twelve openings. It is a square building having three arches on each side. These handsome arches and the four prominent cupolas, one at each corner, combine to present a superb example of the architectural taste of the *Omra* during Shahjahan's period.

During the Sikh period, it served the military purpose when the area was turned into a *Chhowni* or cantonment. During the *Raj,* when the military quarters were shifted to Mian Mir, the *Baradari* served as the Settlement and Post Office. Eventually it became the house of the Punjab Public Library, having also served as part of the Lahore Museum. During 1970s when the Library moved to its new abode just in the vicinity, the *Baradari* was restituted, to be preserved as part of the rich cultural heritage of the city. After carrying out thorough conservation and restoration of the building and its available surroundings, the Pavilion is now open to public as an historical monument.

WAZIR KHAN'S HAMMAM

Inside the Delhi Gate immediately on turning left one encounters an impressive single storey building at the right hand, which presently houses a vocational school and a community centre for the residents of the congested Mohallah. Originally it was a *Hammam* consisting of two blocks different from each other in planning and separated by a passage running in an east-west direction.

From the *Waqf* Deed written in 1641 it is clear that the *Hammam* was a personal property of Nawab Wazir Khan and must have been built earlier. Alongwith shops, *serai* etc. he also bequeathed permanently its income for the support of the Wazir Khan's Mosque and the establishment attached to it.

The northern block which is about one metre higher than the southern one, comprises of a high-domed octagonal hall flanked by smaller ones on its east and west. The hall has four arched entrances, alternated with rectangular recesses. The main hall has a water tank which had been filled and covered under a floor during, possibly Sikh period. It was recovered during recent conservation operations. However, after properly documenting, it has again been covered to keep it in preserved condition and let the modified use of the hall serve the present situation.

The octagonal hall, about 9.5 metres in height, is surmounted by a low dome resting on a high octagonal drum. The top of the dome has a circular opening while each of the faces of the drum has a rectangular opening, all for air and light.

Wazir Khan's Hammam: Partly redone, original fresco paintings.
(Photo courtesy Ian Harper)

The two flanking halls lying in north-south direction, are divided into three bays by means of two transverse arches. Each of the bays has a low dome with circular opening at the top.

The main feature of the southern block is the octagonal hall with an opening in each face. The eastern and the western openings lead in to spacious rooms having domes. The south-western opening leads to a small mosque with *Mihrab* or niche in the western wall.

The access to the roof is from the passage separating the two blocks.

The *Hammam* is built in small size bricks using the bonding material consisting of lime mixed with small pebbles and pieces of burn-bricks. The exterior has cut and dressed bricks with regular recessed panels. The parapet is decorated with *zanjira* pattern in relief. The interior which was earlier white-washed showed beautiful frescoes after carefully removing the upper white layer during recent conservation operations.

Wazir Khan's Hammam: Fresco decoration.
(Photo courtesy Ian Harper)

140

SHAHDARA COMPLEX OF MONUMENTS

With the advent of Islam in the South Asian Subcontinent the impact of a different culture was soon to have its effect on local traditions and traits. Under the Muslim rulers the arts and crafts took a different shape of expression. The Muslims introduced a new class of religious architecture, the tomb, in the Subcontinent where it had been totally unknown due to obvious reasons. This form of Islamic architectural art eventually evolved into such superb examples as the Taj Mahal at Agra and the Mausoleum of Jahangir at Shahdara, Lahore. Few other funerary monuments excelled them in size and architectural splendours in the whole of the world.

The Complex of funerary monuments belonging to the Mughal period, lying at Shahdara consists of three outstanding tombs. The tomb of Jahangir now forms its eastern-most part while that of Asif Khan is in the middle and the tomb of Nurjahan at the western fringe. Situated about 5 kilometres from Lahore, the complex is located near the right bank of the river Ravi, with Shahdara town on its north. It can be approached through either of the two roads branching off respectively from near the Kutcheri and the Sheikhupura crossing on the Grand Trunk Road. The former approach leads one to the Tomb of Nurjahan and then on to the others, through the railway underpass, while the latter is directed straight to the main Gate of *Akbari Serai*, or the forecourt of the Jahangir's Mausoleum.

The son and successor of Emperor Akbar the Great, Jahangir was born in 1569. He ascended the throne in 1605 and after reigning for 22 years, died at Rajauri near Sialkot during one of his sojourns from Kashmir to Lahore. In accordance with his last wish, his body was brought to Lahore and buried in *Dilkusha* Garden at Shahdara.

Jahangir's Tomb: A general view.

141

AKBARI SERAI

The approach to the Jahangir's tomb is through a spacious open court, called *Akbari Serai*. It is mentioned as *Jilau Khana-e-Rauza* or the court attached to the Mausoleum. Its open courtyard is surrounded by cells constructed on raised terrace on all of its four sides. The cells have a veranda and a common passage running all along.

There are two imposing gateways, one each on the northern and southern sides, the latter one presently serving as the main entrance to the complex. A small but beautiful mosque is set in the middle of the western row of the cells. The gateway to the Tomb of Jahangir is towards east, exactly opposite the mosque. The stately gate is a monument in itself. It is decorated with red sandstone richly inlaid with white marble motifs. The half dome of the arch of the gate has attractive honey-comb pendatives flanked by panels representing pinnacles and bunches of flowers.

The *Serai* was used to accommodate the establishment looking after the Mausoleum, in addition to providing a secure halting place to travellers. During the British period, however, it served as a depot of the North Western Railway.

Mosque in Akbari Serai

142

Jahangir's Tomb: Entrance from Akbari Serai

Jahangir's Tomb: Part of the western façade showing
main access and a corner minaret.

144

TOMB OF JAHANGIR

The building of the tomb is set in a luxuriant square garden which was laid in 1557 by a Nawab during the reign of Emperor Akbar. However, it was acquired later by the accomplished queen of Jahangir, Nurjahan, who named it *Dilkusha* and always kept it dearly.

The garden spreads over an area of about 28 hectares. It is on the fashion of the Persian *Charbagh* style, thus dividing it into four quarters which in turn get divided into four, each making the whole standing in sixteen divisions separated by means of richly patterned cut and dressed brick-paved walkways with water channels running in the middle. At each intersection a square or octagonal water tank is provided with a white marble fountain and four red sandstone cascades. The garden is enclosed by a high perimeter wall having gateways in all the four directions.

Based on a square plan, the tomb proper is a single storey building, of comparatively low height, standing on a high platform. The exterior of the building has a facing of red sandstone richly inlaid with white marble decorative motifs mostly in the form of ewer, fruit dish and rose-water sprinkler.

Jahangir's Tomb, main access.

145

The central burial chamber has series of rooms around it. An arched veranda in front of these rooms encircles the whole building. A profusely decorated vaulted-bay leads to the central burial chamber, from each of the four sides. The entrance bay, providing access to the central chamber, is on the western side. It is embellished with beautifully done fresco paintings on the ceiling and the side walls while the mosaic work upto dado level adds grace to the passage.

The sarcophagus, its platform and the floor are all laid in white marble with exquisite *pietra dura* work using cut pieces of various stones like *sang-e-badal, sang-e-abri, sang-e-moosa* and white marble. The cenotaph is a treat to the eye with its beautiful calligraphy done in *pietra dura*. There are ninety nine attributes of Allah on two sides and *Kalima Sharif* at the head. At the foot are given the name and date of death of the Monarch, inscribed in Persian, while on the top is an extract in Arabic from the Holy Quran.

The court historian of Shahjahan tells that there was another cenotaph built in the middle of the spacious roof. This second cenotaph also rested over a platform and was perhaps decorated with marble railing. Neither the cenotaph nor railing can now be found here. The myth of the building having a second storey removed by the Sikhs during eighteenth/nineteenth century is, however, not corroborated from any contemporary written records or the evidence found at the site.

Jahangir's Tomb: A closer view of the facade showing main entrance.

Access to the tomb chamber

A high-rising red sandstone-faced minaret at each corner of the square building adds beauty to its grace. Each of the minarets is crowned with a white marble cupola. The minarets rise in five stages upto a height of over 30 metres and have red sandstone spiral stairs running inside. The minarets are decorated with variegated marble in zig-zag patterns in the middle three stages while a white marble railing, supported over marble brackets, is provided at the top of each stage. The height and the design of the minarets compensate well the otherwise dwarfed look of the building.

Muhammad Saleh Kamboh tells that the mausoleum over the grave of Jahangir was constructed by Emperor Shahjahan, his son and the successor, at a cost of ten lacs of rupees (1,000,000) in ten years.

The magnificent building suffered at the hands of the Sikh rulers between 1767 and 1839 when it was stripped off of its precious decorations to use them elsewhere in Sikh monuments. It served as a residence for M. Amise, a French officer in Ranjit Singh's army. After his death, the Maharaja gave it to Sultan Muhammad Khan, brother of Dost Muhammad Khan, whose followers also played havoc to this monument. During the British *Raj* it served as a railway store depot.

Jahangir's Tomb: Water-channel running over the top of the wall.

148

TOMB OF ASIF KHAN

On the western side of the *Akbari Serai* lies the tomb of Mirza Abul Hasan Asif Jah commonly known as Asif Khan. He was the brother of the gifted queen of Jahangir, Nurjahan, and father of Arjumand Bano Begam, the beloved queen of Shahjahan now lying buried in the Taj Mahal at Agra. Himself a *Wazir* of the Emperor and known for his fabulous wealth, Asif Khan died in 1641. His tomb was erected by Shahjahan at a cost of three lakhs (300,000) of rupees taking a period of four years.

The tomb stands in the middle of a spacious garden with usual water channels, fountains, water reservoirs, walkways, etc. and enclosed by a high wall built in bricks and plastered with lime. The majestic gate lies in the south, though now it remains closed. The present access to the Tomb is through a cell immediately south of the mosque in the *Akbari Serai*.

The tomb building, octagonal in plan, is erected wholly in bricks and rests on an eight-sided platform, the side walls of which were covered with red sandstone. The high bulbous dome and the interior had marble facing. The encaustic or glazed tiles decorated the arched openings. The walls were embellished with inlay work using a variety of stones. The marble cenotaph is beautifully decorated with delicate *pietra dura* work in floral pattern with ninety nine attributes of Allah in *Naskh* script.

The tomb is perhaps one of the most glaring examples of plunder by the Sikhs during the period they held sway over Punjab. The building is now mere shadow of its original grace and glory. Ranjit Singh stripped off all of its marble and other stones, except the damaged cenotaph, to re-use the material in the temple at Amritsar and elsewhere in other buildings.

TOMB OF NURJAHAN

On the western side of the Mausoleum of Asif Khan, across the railway line, lies the tomb of Nurjahan, the accomplished queen of the Emperor Jahangir. She died in 1645, at the age of seventy two, surviving Jahangir by eighteen years. She was buried in this building which she had herself erected during her lifetime.

Standing on a square platform it is a single-storey building, with four main arches, and eight oblong openings in the centre, having three rows of arches beyond.

The original cenotaph was in marble with attributes of Allah engraved on it but the same was robbed during the Sikh period when the marble and other stones decorating the edifice were taken away for re-use in the temple at Amritsar. The building now presents a simple look with two graves - one that of Nurjahan and the other of her daughter, Ladli Begam - in the inner room. Underneath is a chamber enclosing the sepulchres.

The tomb was originally set in a garden on the Persian *Charbagh* pattern which was separated from the Asif Khan's tomb by its western wall. Its main gate was also on the southern side. After the despoliation of the tomb by the Sikhs it was further destroyed and stripped off of its beauty when the Lahore-Rawalpindi railway line was laid through the garden completely detaching it from the adjoining complex, and thus ruining it of its beauty.

TOMB OF ANARKALI

One of the most romantic legends of the Mughal era is Anarkali, literally pomegrenade bud. Though not supported by the contemporary records, the story has been the favourite topic for fiction writers and performing artists.

Anarkali is said to be an attributed name of Nadira Begam or Sharf-un-nisa, a very attractive girl brought up in Akbar's *Harem*. She was suspected by the Emperor of carrying out a secret love-affair with Prince Salim who was to succeed his father to the throne as Emperor Jahangir. The story is differently narrated but the pith of the legend is that she was executed in 1599 for her amorous slip. On ascending the throne six years later, the Prince, now the Emperor Jahangir, built this big and bold monument to her memory.

The mausoleum was completed in 1615 and since has gone under so many changes and alterations that it has lost almost all of its original decorations.

During the reign of Maharaja Ranjit Singh it served as a residential building for his son and successor, Kharak Singh. Subsequently, it was given to General Ventura, the famous Italian officer in the Sikh army, for his residence. During the mid-nineteenth century the building was used as a Christian church when its arched openings were blocked partially or completely. The whole building underwent many changes and was thoroughly

white-washed. It was at this time that the marble cenotaph or *ta'wiz*, was removed from its original place. Later on, when the building was spared the use by religious authorities, the cenotaph was placed in one of the bays where it is still lying. In 1891 the building was converted into the Record Office and still serves as the headquarter of the Punjab Archives.

The cenotaph which is in a single marble piece, is elaborately carved with delicate floral and tendril designs. The calligraphy, lacking uniformity of pen, is carved boldly in *Nasta'liq*. On the top of the slab and the three sides are inscribed the ninety nine attributes of Allah. On the west side of the *Ta'wiz* under the fore-mentioned inscription appears a line mentioning the enamoured Salim (son of) Akbar. There are two dates mentioned in the inscription. One of them gives, in letters and in figures, the year A.H. 1008 (1599) while the other, under the word 'in Lahore' - on the west side of the sacrophagus - is A.H. 1024 (1615). The first one probably refers to the year of death of Anarkali while the latter gives the date of the building of the tomb.

GULABI BAGH GATEWAY

On the way from Lahore city to the Shalamar Garden, rather closer to the latter, the Gateway to the *Gulabi Bagh* or Garden of Roses, lies on the left side of the present Grand Trunk Road. It was built in 1655 by a Persian nobleman, Mirza Sultan Beg, Admiral of the Fleet and a cousin of the husband of Sultan Begam, daughter of Shahjahan. He was fond of sport and was killed on a shooting expedition through the bursting of an English fire-arm given to him by the Emperor.

The name *Gulabi Bagh* actually serves as to giving the chronogram, the numerical value of the letters expressing the date when building was constructed and the garden laid out. According to *Hijra* calendar it gives the year as 1066. The inscriptions reads as:-

محمّد عربی کابر وی ہر دو سرا است

کسی کہ خاک درش نیست خاک بر سراو

خوش آن باغی کہ دارد لالہ دا غش   بانی باغ سخاوت فاتح باب کرم

کلی خورشید و مہ زبیدہ چراغش   آنکہ از دارای گردوس ساخت باغ چوں ارم

ز تقویم خرد پرسید غازی   اہل معنی بر دو مش خواستند از حق دُعا

گلابی باغ شد تاریخ باغش   بیگ سلطان الہی دارد دائم محترم

ھ ۱۰۶۶

The translation of the inscription is as under:-

*What a pleasant garden, a garden so beautiful that the poppy is marked with the black spot (the spot of envy). The flowers of the sun and moon are fitted to adorn it as lamps. Ghazi asked of wisdom the chronogram of the garden. The date given was **Gulabi Bagh**.*

The Gateway is a simple square building with the usual high half-domed central arch flanked on each side by multi-cusp head in the upper stage. The angles are marked by slender octagonal minaret-like pilasters. The notable feature of the structure is its mosaic tile decoration, which is still well-preserved on the outer face and is a good example of the achievement of the Lahori tile-workers of the mid-seventeenth century. Apart from the spandrels, which contain the usual floral tendrils, the design consists of floral or inscriptional panels with raised brick frames plastered and painted with imitation brick-work or *tazakari*. Yellow is a dominant colour, as it was liable to be at this period, but green, brown, blue and white combine to produce a rich and varied effect which is further strengthened by the mosaic technique.

Gulabi Bagh Gateway

153

DAI ANGA'S TOMB

Behind the *Gulabi Bagh* Gateway on the site of the former garden, stands the tomb of *Dai* Anga, Shahjahan's wet-nurse. Her daughter also lies buried in the same tomb which is of brick and stands upon a podium covering the actual burial vault. It is square on plan, with a flattened central dome and a pavilion at each corner. The dome is tiled in white and dark blue zigzag pattern. The tall cylindrical drum is decorated with floral pattern in mosaic tiles in which green and yellow predominate. The domes of the pavilions were also tiled but for the rest these are plastered and painted. The cresting of the main building is also tiled, with a tiled string-course below which the walls are panelled and plastered, and were formerly painted. The interior of the dome is plastered, with painted interlaced ribbing or tracery, and is carried on honey-combed squinches. The grave stones have disappeared. An inscription in the tomb-chamber gives a date equivalent to 1671.

Dai Anga's Tomb

TOMB OF ALI MARDAN KHAN

On the southern side of the Grand Trunk Road, opposite *Gulabi Bagh* Gateway lies the imposing tomb of Ali Mardan Khan. He was the same outstanding Canal Engineer of Shahjahan, who made it possible to bring the water of the Ravi to Shalamar Garden at a level higher than the corresponding bed of the river where its main stream flowed, resulting in the great feat of a three-terrace landscape with decorative canals, fountains, cascades etc. and beautifully green lawns, shrubs and fruit trees.

The lofty tomb is octagonal in shape, and surrounded by a platform. Originally covered with variegated and red sandstone, the tomb hardly bears that lavish decoration, thanks to the ruthless hands of the Sikhs. The building once stood in the midst of a walled garden which is no more to be seen except the remains of a gateway. In the underground room, under the central dome are interned the mortal remains of the great genius.

The Gateway is quite expansive in size and richly decorated with glazed tiles of various colours. The façade of the Gate has painted alcoves.

The building of the tomb was used in the time of Maharaja Ranjit Singh as a military magazine while the Gateway structure served as a private residence of a Sikh army's general.

Tomb of Ali Mardan Khan.

NADIRA BEGAM'S TOMB

In close proximity to the mausoleum of Hazrat Mian Mir, the famous saint, lies a very odd tomb of the Mughal period. Unlike other contemporary funerary architectural accomplishments it is not raised within a formal garden. Instead, it stands in the centre of a large tank. In the absence of a dome it looks more like a pavilion than a tomb, in which lies the peculiarity of its architecture.

In this *baradari*—like tomb structure are interned the mortal remains of Princess Nadira Begam, wife of Prince Dara Shikoh, the eldest son of Shahjahan and a brother of Aurangzeb Alamgir. She herself was the daughter of Prince Pervaiz, the second son of the Emperor Jahangir. On mother's side she also claimed the royal lineage, being the grand daughter of Prince Murad, son of Emperor Akbar the Great. Nadira's marriage, first postponed because of the death of the Empress Mumtaz Mahal, was finally solemnised in Agra in 1634.

Nadira Begam was a devoted wife and accompanied her husband in his destitute wanderings in Sindh, and exile, during his unsuccessful struggle for the throne against his younger brother Moheyuddin, the Emperor Aurangzeb Alamgir. Though bearing the hardships with courage and patience she finally succumbed to fatigue and diarrhoea and died on 6th June, 1659 at Dhadar at the mouth of the Bolan Pass. Her dead body was sent to Lahore, under the charge of Khwaja Ma'qul with an escort of seventy soldiers, to be buried, in accordance with her last wish, in the graveyard of the Great Saint, Mian Mir.

The tomb over her grave was probably built by Aurangzeb Alamgir. The building lies in the centre of a large tank and is provided with an access through causeway, 1.75 metres wide, on its eastern side. The plinth of the tomb rests about three metres above the floor of the tank. The two-storied simple building is square in plan, each side measuring about 13.4 metres and rising to a total height of 9.90 metres. Built in burnt-brick with kankar lime mortar, the pavilion is a *baradari* having three recessed openings on each side. The central openings bear arches and are flanked by flat smaller vestibules. Both of the storeys are exactly the same in design and extent.

The grave lies in the middle of the pavilion. On its northern side *Bismillah sharif* and *Kalima Tayyaba,* in *Nasta'liq,* are inlaid in marble. At the southern side the inscription in the same style gives the name and date of death of the Princess.

The interior of both the storeys, as also the ceiling and faces of all the walls, is decorated with traditional *Ghalib-kari* panels of various geometrical designs. The dado of the upper-storey, however, bears traces of brilliantly-done multi-coloured glazed tile work.

Two narrow stairs, one from the south-east and the other from south west, lead to the roof which is flat except an hexagonal platform of about 0.7 metres height, which is placed in the centre.

The tank around the pavilioned tomb was once enclosed by a wall. With a gateway each on its north and south, the tank was square in shape - each side measuring about 177 metres. The causeway providing access to the main tomb bears 32 arched openings, the 33rd in the middle having been closed to form a beautiful square platform.

The monument, like many others in Lahore, did not escape the vandalism of the Sikhs when during their short reign they removed the choicest material from the structure.

SARV WALA MAQBRA

The *Sarv Wala Maqbra*, literally meaning the Cypress Tomb, lies not far from the Dai Anga's Tomb. However, the modern construction of residential colony in its surroundings has not only detached it from the latter but also marred it of the whole of its beauty as according to Muhammad Latif, it was surrounded by a garden which did exist during his period.

The building is a tomb of Sharfunnisa Begam, a sister of Nawab Zakariya Khan (d. 1745), the viceroy of Lahore during the reign of Mughal ruler Muhammad Shah (719 - 48).

It is a solid, tower-like structure in brick, tapering upwards. It has a *Chhajja* (pent) near the top, surmounted by a four-sided pyramidal low dome carried over a double, though low, neck. The square burial chamber is on the top, at a height of about 5 metres.

The edifice takes its name *Sarv Wala Maqbra*, from its ornamentation of cypress (*sarv*) trees. The cypresses, four on each side are intercepted by smaller blooming flower plants, all done in enamelled tile mosaic work on plaster base.

Serv Wala Maqbra

158

BUDDHU KA AWA

A very stately brick-kiln of Lahore, known as *Buddhu ka Awa* lies on the southern side of the Grand Trunk Road, on way to Shalamar. The kiln is ascribed to the son of Suddhu who was a potter during the reign of Shahjahan. Suddhu himself built a number of kilns under the royal patronage, for supplying burnt bricks to build the edifices by the royalty and palaces by the *Omra* of the court. It is said that the fires in the kiln extinguished for ever as a result of a curse from a *Faqir* who was denied to benefit from the warmth of the kiln fire in a cold wet day.

During the period of Maharaja Ranjit Singh his French General, Avitabile, built a summer house on the remains of the kiln, though no trace of it is anymore found on the site. It was also used to collect at this spot the *Khalsa* (Sikh) troops by Maharaja Sher Singh and Raja Hira Singh to lay siege on Lahore.

Buddhu's Tomb

Chauburji

CHAUBURJI

The delicately lofty building standing alone in an island of traffic on the Multan Road is now commonly known as *Chauburji* because of its having four (*chau*) minarets (*burji*). Originally it was a gateway to the garden of Zebunnisa, or Zebinda Begam, the accomplished daughter of Aurangzeb. The garden is believed to have extended from Nawankot in the south to the main city of Lahore towards north. However, no remains of such an expansive garden are now traceable.

A fragmentary inscription on the eastern archway records that the garden was built in A.H. 1056 *i.e.* 1646. According to this inscription it was built by *Sahib-e-Zebinda* (one endowed with elegance), *Begam-e-Dauran* (the lady of the age) and was bestowed upon Mian Bai, Fakhrunnisa (the pride of the ladies).

فنا پذیرش داین باغ روضه رضوان بجشت
این باغ زروضه رضوان بجشت مرحمت باغ
از میا یا بُی زلطف صاحب زبیده بیگم دوراں
ساخت میا یا بی فخرنسا روضه عالی ارم احتشام

The building is richly decorated with brilliantly executed enamelled tiles in blue and green, and frescoes of excellent beauty. The corner towers or *burji*, look slender for their height and reached to the top ending up in covered platform which carried arched pavilions.

The *Ayat-ul-Kursi* from the Holy Quran is inscribed in the blue enamelled letters in the panel over the main vault. The *Hijra* year 1056 is given at its end.

One of the minarets on the north western side had given way long time ago. In order to restore the logical look of *Chauburji*, the Department of Archaeology and Museums carried out some conservation and restoration works in the late 1960s. Thus after rebuilding the fourth *burji*, minaret, the monument has regained some of its old glory.

NAWANKOT MONUMENTS

Nawankot had been a fortified quarter of Lahore, though about five kilometres south of the Walled City. The fort, considerable remains of which still exist, was raised in brick by Mahar Mohkam in 1763. The garden once laid out at this site is traditionally attributed to Mian Bai, on whom the *Chauburji* Gateway and the adjoining garden was bestowed by, probably, Jahan Ara Begam, the eldest daughter of the Emperor Shahjahan. Presently a gateway, towers and a tomb remind of the past grandeur of the place.

A. The Gateway:

Constructed in cut-brick work, the lofty Gateway has a three-centred high central arch. Above the plinth and below the cresting of crenellated *kanguras,* it is embellished with enamelled tile-mosaic. The interior of the gateway is decorated with fresco paintings in beautiful floral designs. The green, blue, yellow and orange colours dominate in the mosaic work while in the fresco paintings green and red colours are more pronounced. The four small corner pavilions at the top have fluted domes carried over brick-built slender pillars.

B. The Corner Towers:

With a girth of considerable dimensions the two corner-towers are octagonal on plan. Each of them is surmounted by an octagonal domed pavilion with eight arched openings. The domes have flutes formed in golden yellow enamelled terracotta tiles. These towers (*burjs)* once formed respectively the north-eastern and south-eastern corners of the now extinct garden.

C. The Tomb:

A little distance west of the Nawankot Gateway, amidst modern houses, lies the stripped brick core of the undated tomb. It is, however, attributed to Zebunnisa, the learned daughter of the Emperor Aurangzeb Alamgir. It is said that after making the gift of the garden at *Chauburji* to her maid-servant, Mian Bai, the princess laid out an extensive garden at the spot of Nawankot. She adorned this garden with buildings. In the garden she also constructed a mausoleum for herself, wherein she was buried after her death.

The tomb is square on plan and has two graves placed on a brick-platform. A portion of the original tessellated floor has survived the Sikh vandalism. These patches of *sang-e-Badal* flooring match well with that found in the veranda of Jahangir's Tomb.

The pyramidal dome, curvilinear externally and hemispherical internally, is a specimen of its own class.

Gateway of the Nawankot.

Glazed Tiled Panel gateway of Nawankot, southren side.

Tomb of Zebunnisa

Detail of Nawankot Gateway.

Baradari in Huzuri Bagh.

SIKH CONTRIBUTION

BARADARI IN HAZURI BAGH

One of the buildings of merit constructed during the Sikh reign in Lahore is the white marble *Baradari* of Ranjit Singh. Located in the middle of the *Hazuri Bagh* with the gigantic Alamgiri Gate on one side and the gorgeous Badshahi *Masjid* Entrance on the other, the grandeur of the *Baradari* has been over-shadowed and its stature dwarfed to a great extent. Built originally in double-storey, it is perhaps the only outstanding architectural achievement of the Sikhs - and that more by chance than design - which has added to its eventful history by being partially demolished by heavy rains in the late 1920s.

The *Baradari* was constructed at the order of Maharaja Ranjit Singh in the year 1818. Though an artistic success, it is also a monument of vandalism. The material of which it was constructed had been obtained by despoiling tombs and monuments of the bygone age of the Mughals. The opinions may differ as to the exact source of the material but even a cursory look at the arrangement of some of the stones will speak loud of the brutality with which Ranjit Singh might have treated the Mughal master-pieces of architectural art.

The famous historian of Lahore, Syed Muhammad Latif asserts that the material for the *Baradari* came from the demolished tomb of Zebunnisa Begam at Nawankot and the once sumptuous tomb of Muhammad Sharif which stood near the Taxali Gate. It seems quite possible in the face of the fact that many other ancient tombs and edifices were ruthlessly despoiled by the Maharaja to erect or decorate his own buildings.

There has also been a general opinion that the whole structure once stood on the roof of Jahangir's tomb at Shahdara, covering the opening above the tomb of the Emperor. It had been, in a way, transplanted in the central place of the *Hazuri Bagh* at the orders of Maharaja Ranjit Singh. This theory has, however, generally been dispelled by those who collated and analysed all the available material.

During his life-time the pavilion remained a favourite resort of Ranjit Singh for pleasure and business when he was tired of walled fort or the *Shamiana* he often used. Here, in simple state, he sat amid his courtiers and soldiers dispensing the rude and speedy justice of the period or conducted state business under the respectful eyes of the citizens who thronged the *Hazuri Bagh* to pay homage or feel the honour of the nearness to the presence of the founder of the Sikh rule. These were the peaceful days of the marble *Baradari* ending with his death, for almost immediately commenced that long period of civil and military strife and confusion usually called as the Great Anarchy. During these days the pavilion stood serene in the midst of war, murder, assassination and plunder.

After about three months of the death of Maharaja Ranjit Singh, and that of his son, Naunihal Singh who had succeeded his father for just few hours, Sher Singh besieged the Lahore Fort with about 30,000 troops to regain the throne which had been robbed by *Mai* Chand Kaur. After the Fort had been surrounded on three sides, Sher Singh took up his position in the marble pavilion of the *Hazuri Bagh* and received allegiance of all those who "sat on the fence". After a three days' siege Gulab Singh surrendered the Fort on honourable terms after besiegers had suffered 1,800 casualties, most of them fell in the *Hazuri Bagh* between the marble pavilion and the Alamgiri Gate.

Like his predecessors, Sher Singh made much use of the marble pavilion. In the assembly of leading *Sirdars*, *darbaries* and citizens of Lahore it was in this Pavilion that he declared the child, procured by Chand Kaur, as the son and true heir of the late Naunihal Singh.

A few months after the death of Sher Singh, Pertab Singh and Dhian Singh were assassinated. Within few hours of their deaths Hira Singh, son of Dhian Singh, aroused the troops to execute his vengeance, and once more the Fort of Lahore was besieged and the city given up to plunder and outrage. For two days Hira Singh sat within the marble pavilion stimulating the besiegers to increase efforts by bribes of money and gold bracelets. The breach came at last and the storming besiegers put to death the whole garrison of about one thousand. The heads of the murderers of the three great were laid at the feet of Hira Singh in this Pavilion.

Sikh Baradari in original condition.
(Photo courtesy Department of Archaeology & Museum, Pakistan).

The now peaceful-seeming edifice perhaps witnessed this all as the last barbarously bloody tragedy. Just a few months later, Hira Singh too fell a victim to the plots of his enemies and fled from the city but was put to death by his pursuers.

After this episode the marble Pavilion no more appears in the accounts of historians, perhaps it was too dangerous to hold open *Darbar* and state assemblies during the Sikh rule ever after.

The floors and some other parts of the Pavilion are of commoner material, sometime differing from stone to stone. The ceilings are decorated with pieces of crude mirror glass in rustic style peculiar to the Sikhs.

As the centre of magnificent scenes, the pavilion is mentioned by visitors to Lahore, during the times of Sikh Maharajas. Among these were Burnes, Hugel, Prince Soltykof and Count von Ohrlich of the Prussian Guard. The latter writes an interestingly scenic account of the *Darbar* in the marble pavilion.

SIKH COMPLEX OF MONUMENTS

Opposite the Lahore Fort towards west of the Postern Gate a large modern compound wall encloses in it some of the important monuments of the Sikh period. The major historical buildings of the Complex are the *Smadhs* of Maharaja Ranjit Singh, Kharak Singh and Naunihal Singh, a marble *baradari*, Shrine of Arjan Mal, etc.

SMADH OF MAHARAJA RANJIT SINGH

The *Smadh* or the mausoleum of the Sikh Maharaja Ranjit Singh is an admixture of Hindu and Muslim architecture. It is built of stone in a plain style boasting of no architectural grandeur. In addition to some of the Hindu dieties in red sandstone, on the front entrance, the ceiling of the building is decorated with small convex mirrors set in white marble. A lotus flower carved in marble and set beneath a canopy, serves to cover the ashes of the Maharaja. The other smaller flowers of similar nature are said to represent his four wives and seven slave-girls who immolated themselves, in *Satti* tradition, on the funeral pyre of their deceased master.

The building of the *Smadh* was started by Kharak Singh but could not be completed due to his death. Sher Singh continued the work but it could be completed only during the later period of Dilip Singh.

Marble *Baradari:*

The marble *baradari* of Devi in one of the chambers in fact belonged to Maharani Jindan, the beloved wife of Maharaja Ranjit Singh. She made this gift to the *Smadh* at the time of her removal from Lahore.

Other *Smadhs:*

The two buildings, of unpretentious nature, with small domes lying on the farther side of the *Smadh* of Ranjit Singh are the memorials containing ashes of Kharak Singh and Naunihal Singh, respectively the son and the grandson of the Maharaja Ranjit Singh.

Ranjit Singh's Smadh.

SHRINE OF GURU ARJAN MAL

The next to the *Smadh* of Ranjit Singh towards its east is the Shrine of Arjan Mal, the fifth Guru of the Sikhs. He is responsible for re-arranging the sacred writings of earlier Gurus. This work came to be known as *Adi-Granth* and forms the basic part of Sikh scriptures. He also raised Amritsar to the Sikh religion's focal point.

The *Guru* was alleged of favouring the party of Emperor Jahangir's rebellious son, Prince Khusrow who for some time had managed to hold sway over Punjab. He was arrested and prisoned by the Emperor and is believed to have died of the rigours though his followers believe that after having obtained permission to bathe in the river Ravi he miraculously disappeared under the waters. The *Smadh* was later built by Maharaja Ranjit Singh at the spot of his miraculous disappearance.

SIKH ART TREASURES IN LAHORE FORT

Maharaja Ranjit Singh came to power in 1799 after a turbulent rule of three Sikh Chiefs and then a very brief occupation of Lahore by the Durrani king, Shah Zambian. Ranjit Singh was able to consolidate his kingdom through his shrewdness and skilful handling of the affairs. After his death in 1839, the internal strife and conspiracies in his successors resulted in a few very short-lived rules. Finally his youngest son, Dalip Singh, was proclaimed Maharaja in 1843 when he was only six years of age. The ensuing Sikh wars with the *Raj* army ended in complete annihilation of the Sikh rule. Their kingdom was ultimately annexed to the British India in 1849 and the young Maharaja was removed to Fatehgarh in the United Province. Later, he was granted a pension and sent to England where he was given an estate in Suffolk. He married the daughter of a European merchant and had six children, all of whom died issueless.

Princess Bamba Jindan Dalip Singh, the third child of the deposed Maharaja outlived all her brothers and sisters. She inherited, among other things, a marvellous collection of paintings and *objets d'art* belonging to her father. She died at Lahore in 1957, without an heir. She bequeathed the collection to Pir Karim Bakhsh Supra, her trusted attending driver. In view of the historical and artistic value of the collection, the Government of Pakistan acquired it from the Pir and put it on exhibition in the Lahore Fort.

The collection originally belonged to Maharaja Ranjit Singh and seems to have been moved to England where young Maharaja Dalip Singh lived in exile. The collection comprises of 88 objects and includes oil paintings, water colours, ivory paintings, models cast in metal, photographs and miscellaneous objects. The collection speaks in ample terms about the life and time during the respective reigns of Maharajas Ranjit Singh and Dalip Singh. In addition to the distinct depiction of the Sikh *Darbar* or court, it tells of the artistic taste of the Sikh royalty during the 19th century.

An interesting aspect of the paintings in the collection is that most of these are the works of European artists and painters like August Schoefft, Leslie Poole Smith, Goldingham, Blakeney Ward, P.C.French, Paillet and Winterhalter. As such they mainly represent the European style of the 19th century and hardly have any resemblance to the Sikh style of painting which generally followed the Kangra School.

Amongst the paintings, the one depicting the 'Darbar of Maharaja Ranjit Singh' by August Shoefft attracts the eye immediately on entering the upper storey in the gallery. It is painted on an exceptionally large-sized canvas, 4.9 x 2.5 metres, and portrays the minute details of the *Darbar*. The locale of the scene is the Sikh period marble pavilion, *Athdara*, adjoining the *Shish Mahal* in the Fort of Lahore. The Maharaja himself is seen receiving *nazrana*. He is surrounded by the members of the royal family, courtiers nobles and high officials of the state including the European officers of his army. It may be of interest to point out that prior to its shifting to Pakistan this very painting remained on display in the British Museum, London, for some time.

The other paintings deserving special attention are the ones showing 'Ranjit Singh at Amritsar' and 'Sher Singh in Council'. The oil paintings in the collection also include the portraits of the last Mughal Emperor Bahadur Shah and his two sons in addition to that of Dalip Singh.

While the oil paintings have a stamp of the European style, all the twenty two, oval-shaped, ivory miniature paintings depict the style in vogue in the South Asian Subcontinent, particularly Delhi, Agra and Benaras in the 19th century. These paintings were executed by some artist of Punjab but his name does not appear with any of his creations. These miniature paintings are beautifully arranged in six rows, four paintings in each of the upper five rows, depicting different personages. The sixth or the bottom row contains two paintings, one of them portraying the Shalamar Garden while the other showing the Taj Mahal.

An exquisitely done model of Ranjit Singh riding-in-state is another object of special mention. It is made of silver and measures 81 cm. in length 58 in breadth and 112 in height. Ranjit Singh is shown sitting in a delicately worked *Hauda* on an elephant, with an attendant sitting in the rear and holding the royal umbrella. The pedestal and the plinth of the model depict an assortment of soldiers, horses and other scenes with animals and beasts.

The rich horse-trappings belonging to Ranjit Singh also make part of the display. They appear in a separate room, adorning a taxidermized white horse to give them a real-life look. The trappings consist of three pieces: *Sar Band, Seena Band* and *Dum Gazz* or tail strap. They are covered with red velvet, richly set in gold decoration and studded with diamonds, rubies, jaspers, etc. The original gold plated royal umbrella is also there to complete the story of the grandeur and wealths of Maharaja who also possessed the great *Koh-i-Noor* diamond which had been a pride of the Mughal throne.

Maharani Jindan: Canvas (142.24 x 114.3 cm)

172

Darbar of Maharaja Ranjit Singh (c.1838)
by Aug. Schoefft. (canvas, 488x254 cm)

Maharaja Sher Singh.
by Aug. Schoefft. (canvas, 142x113 cm)

Fredrick Dalip Singh in childhood.
By Capt. Goldingham. (canvas 142x105 cm)

Raja Gulab Singh, First
Dogra Chief of Kashmir. (Water colour)

H.H. Maharaja Dalip Singh.
By Capt. Goldingham (Canvas 198x137 cm)

Maharaja Rinjit Singh at Amritsar
by Aug. Schoefft (Canvas, 144x109 cm

Maharaja Sher Singh in council.
by Aug. Schoefft. (Canvas, 61x46 cm)

NATIONAL MONUMENTS
OF MODERN ERA

As is mentioned elsewhere, the city of Lahore mainly saw development being taking place on its southern and south-eastern side during the *Raj* or the Colonial Period. The buildings of this period were generally of utilitarian nature and had their own character separate from the style of the earlier periods of the area. After independence the architectural development continued. Some of the buildings constructed during the Modern Period got the status of National Monuments hence merit specific mention. Among these landmarks are a) Tomb of Allama Muhammad Iqbal, who conceived the idea of a separate motherland for the Muslims of the British India, and b) Minar-e-Pakistan, commemorating the passing of the Lahore Resolution - now commonly known as Pakistan Resolution - which paved the path for ultimate independence on 14 August, 1947.

ALLAMA IQBAL'S TOMB

A small red sandstone building occupies the south-western corner of the *Hazuri Bagh*. Flanked by the towering *Badshahi Masjid* and the awesome Fort, this building presents a unique grandeur in its modesty. Here lies buried Allama Dr. Sir Muhammad Iqbal, the poet-philosopher of the East, and a national hero of Pakistan, who is responsible for giving Muslims of South Asia a definite direction to achieve their identity as a free nation.

Born at Sialkot in 1877, the Allama was one of those few great men who rose to the heights of fame during their life-times. His love of Islam and Muslim culture formed the basis of his philosophy and political thought for the propagation of which he used poetry as a prime medium. His first poetic work in Persian language, *Israr-e-Khudi* was published in 1915. Its English translation by Professor Nicholson appeared in 1920 under the title of "Secrets of Self" and was instrumental in introducing the calibre of the Allama to Europe. This was followed by a number of publications in poety and prose, presenting to the world his philosophical thoughts.

Although the Allama participated a little in the active politics, in its general sense, yet he never stayed out of the main current. He was elected to the Punjab Assembly in 1926 and remained its member till 1930. He was also elected the President of All India Muslim League Session at Allahabad, held in 1930. It was here that in his presidential address he put forward for the first time the idea of a separate homeland for the Muslims of the British India. The same idea became the express aspiration of the Indian Muslims and formed the spirit of the Lahore Resolution passed on 23rd March, 1940, in the famous session of the All India Muslim League presided over by the Quaid-e-Azam Muhammad Ali Jinnah. The dream was realized in concrete shape with the creation of independent Pakistan on the 14th August, 1947.

The Allama suffered protracted physical ailments during the last years of his life. He breathed his last in the morning of 21st April, 1938, at his residence, *Jawed Manzil* on the Mayo Road (now re-named Allama Iqbal Road) in Lahore. The news of his demise spread far and wide in no time and people, including eminent personalities, started gathering at his residence. One of his close friends, and a notable Muslim Leaguer, Chaudhry Muhammad Hussain selected, for his burial, a site which should truly represent the place of the Poet-Philosopher in history. The spot chosen by him was situated by the main entrance of the famous *Badshahi Masjid* built by Emperor Aurangzeb Alamgir in 1674. The particular piece of land came within the Protected Area under the Ancient Monuments Preservation Act-1904 (since replaced by the Antiquities Act-1975). As such necessary permission for the grave was obtained from the Department of Archaeology. The body of the Allama was brought to the site in an unprecedented procession and was laid to eternal rest the same evening.

Soon after, an "Iqbal Tomb Committe" was formed with the main task of constructing a building over his grave that would be worthy of the name of the great man. The Chief Architect of Deccan, Nawab Zain Yar Jang, prepared a design for the tomb, but it was not approved as in the opinion of the Committee it did not fully reflect the character and thought of the Allama. The remarks of the President of the Committe, which were to serve as guideline, are worth

Allama Iqbal's Tomb

quoting: "Here lies the great Mosque, the symbol of our spiritual power, there stands the Fort, the symbol of our temporal power and on that side to the north (Ranjit Singh's *Smadh)* is the rebel. Here lies buried the *Mujaddid.* The design of his mausoleum should aim at the expression in stone of *Khudi,* the Self, its tenacity and power." Another hint was to avoid copying Mughal architectural design as it would not let the building come out in its surroundings. The Committe suggested to draw inspiration from Afghan architecture or, alternately, follow a Moorish design. Nawab Zain Yar Jang was invited to visit the site personally and then prepare the design which should properly fit in the present site without compromising with the basic requirement outlined by the Committee. Consequently he presented design which was the admixture of Afghan and Moorish archtitectural styles. The design was approved by the Committee which decided that 'it would not be a fitting homage to the great poet to erect his mausoleum from funds received from the rulers or contributed by the government.' The funds were to be raised from contributions from the poet's friends, disciples and admirers.

Due to certain technical reasons the work on the construction of the tomb could not be taken in hand for about eight years. It was started in 1946 and completed by 1953-54. In its construction selected red sandstone from Jaipur and marble from Makrana, Rajputana, were used. The *ta'wiz* of the tomb is in Lapislazuli, the most expensive architectural stone found in Afghanistan. It was gifted by the Afghan government. The *ta'wiz* and inscription were prepared in Afghanistan and sent to Lahore in parts to be re-assembled at the site. Two of the *Masha'ls* (torches), however, were damaged during transit with the result that these could not be replaced hence their absence at the southern side. The translucent stone cost over Rs.100,000 in those days. The *ta'wiz* bears the superb specimen of calligraphy represented by *ayaat* taken

Allama Iqbal's Tomb illuminated at night.

181

from the Holy Quran and very aptly chosen couplets from the works of the Allama. On the inner side of the mausoleum wall are written six couplets from a *ghazal* taken from one of the poetic collections of the Allama, namely *Zabur-e-Ajam.*

Although the mausoleum has always remained a great attraction for the dignitaries and the general public who visit it to pay homage to the great poet and philosopher, yet the limited space of the premises did not leave much choice to conduct formal ceremonies. It was only in 1977, the centennial of the great man, that work on its expansion was carried out. A very suitable plan was drawn to build and enlarge the platform around the tomb and provide it with four kiosks for the armed ceremonial guard. The design of the kiosks is kept in line with that of the *mazar* and in complete harmony with the surroundings. To make the expansion look homogenous with the tomb, same type of red sandstone has been used for extending the premises and in building the kiosks.

Allama Iqbal's Tomb with Badshahi Mosque Minaret.

MINAR-E-PAKISTAN

The *Minar-e-Pakistan* or the Tower of Pakistan stands in the Iqbal Park, Lahore at the place where Pakistan Resolution was passed in the historic meeting held on the 22-24 March, 1940. The meeting was presided over by the great leader, *Quaid-e-Azam* Muhammad Ali Jinnah, in which the decision to have a separate and independent homeland for the Muslims of the Subcontinent, was announced.

The construction of the *Minar* was entrusted to the Pakistan Day Memorial Committee with late Nasir-ud-din Murath Khan, a Turkish architect, as its member. The foundation stone was laid on 23rd March, 1960, and the memorial completed on 31st October, 1968, at a cost of Rs.7,058,000.

The *Minar* constructed with different stones obtained from the various parts of Pakistan rests on the base built in the shape of a flower with ten petals. The first storey of the *Minar* is a circular room finished with marble facing. On this are written the ninety-nine attributes of Allah, verses from the Holy Quran, the text of the Pakistan Resolution and short history of Pakistan Movement. Above this room the *Minar* rises through stages, to a height of 59 metres. A lift has been provided to go right up to the top which is crowned by a domelet made of stainless steel.

Badshahi Mosque

Summit Minar, WAPDA House at the background.

Quaid-e-Azam Library

Assembly Hall

Railway Station

Jinnah Hall (Town Hall)

Alhamra

Cultural Complex

Lahore Museum

Government College

Punjab University: Old Campu

Punjab University: New Campus

Queen Victoria's Pavilion.

Monument of Kalma Chowk, Ferozpur Road.

Siggianwala Ravi Bridge

State Bank of Pakistan.

EPILOGUE

The architectural accomplishments of the Mughal period in Lahore by far surpass those of any other period not only in grandeur and magnitude but also in numerical strength. No wonder then that the city often stands identified with that single period of history. During the Sikh period, many buildings of note were constructed but they mostly represented crude taste in style or decoration. In addition to the few already mentioned, some *Havelis* representing this period still stand within the walled city. The *Haveli* of Naunihal Singh, a lofty building constructed by the son of Kharak Singh for his private residence, now accommodates a government girls high school. It has recently been renovated by the Lahore Development Authority under a World Bank Scheme. Another *Haveli*, and a *Smadh*, situated in Hira Mandi not far from the Fort belonged to Dhian Singh, a minister of Ranjit Singh.

About hundred years of the *Raj* saw altogether a different attitude towards architecture and town-planning in Lahore. Out of the thirty-six *guzars* or quarters into which the ancient city was divided, only nine were included within the area of the city when Thornton visited Lahore. On the advent of the British rule, the suburbs of the city lay in ruins of the old buildings, gateways etc. Most of the material from these fallen buildings was re-used and the scene of crumbling monuments turned into 'fine gardens, grassy plains, metalled roads, lined on either side with shady trees, canals, public offices and picturesque European houses.'

The city was extended and expanded on systematic plan. New areas of shopping, trade and residence came up as also a cantonment. Some of the distinct buildings constructed during the British period include the Assembly Chambers, the Governor House, Montgomery (now Jinnah) Hall, Railway Station, the Masonic Hall, Punjab University, Government College, Victoria Jubilee (now only) Town Hall, Mayo School (now National College) of Arts, Museum, etc. The best of the land-scaped areas is the Lawrence (now Jinnah) garden.

After independence on 14th August, 1947, Lahore continued as the capital of the part of Punjab that came to Pakistan. It then served as the seat of the government of the new province of West Pakistan on the unification, in 1956, of all the provinces forming the western wing of the country. However, in 1970, on the formation of the four provinces out of the West Pakistan Province - Punjab, Sindh, Balochistan and the North West Frontier - it reverted to its earlier status of the capital city of Punjab.

It has flourished ever more during the recent years. Dozens of satellite colonies, co-operative housing societies and other area-development schemes have taken its peripheral limits to over tens of kilometres on almost all the sides of the old city. Some of the new landmarks like Minar-e-Pakistan (already mentioned above) *Al Hamra*, Wapda House, Summit *Minar*, Fortress and Gaddafi Stadia etc. have dominated the sky-line of the 'new' Lahore. The building activity, though more of practical nature, still continues to further enrich the architectural format of Lahore.

SELECT BIBLIOGRAPHY

Amin, Muhammad,	Lahore, Lahore, 1988
Baqir, Muhammad,	Lahore: Capital of West Pakistan, Lahore, 1963
Baqir, Muhammad,	Lahore, Past and Present, Lahore, 1984.
Bernier, Francois:	Travels in the Mughal Empire (French: Voyages contenant et al description des Etats du Grand Mogal) Lahore, 1894.
Beveridge, H., (Eng. Tr.)	The Akbar Nama - 3 Vols. Calcutta, 1920.
Balochmann, H., (Eng. Tr.)	The Aine Akbari Vol.I Calcutta, 1873.
Burnes, Alexander,	Travel in Bokhara, 3 Vols. London, 1834.
Caine, W.S.,	Picturesque India London, 1898.
Cole, H.H.	Preservation of National Monuments, in Journal of Indian Art, Vol. VI (1896).
Cope, Henry,	Public inscriptions of Lahore, in Journal of the Asiatic Society of Bengal, Vol. XXVII.
Crooke, William and Ball, C.,	Travels in India by Jean Baptist Travernier, 2 Vols. London, 1925.
Cunnigham, Alexander	Ancient Geography of India, Calcutta, 1924.
Cunnigham, J.D.,	History of the Sikhs, Oxford, 1918.

Derby, J., (Eng. Tr.)	Zafarnama. London, 1723.
De, B., (Eng. Tr.)	Tabaqat-e-Akbari, Calcutta.
Edib, Halide,	Inside India, London, 1938.
Elias, N. and Ross E. Denison (Eng. Tr.)	Tarikh-e- Rashidi
Elphinston, M.,	An Account of Kingdom of Caubul. London, 1815.
Evans Lloyd, H. (Eng. Tr.)	Travels in India including Sinde and the Punjab by Orlich.
Foster, Sir William,	Embassy of Sir Thomas Roe to India. London, 1926.
Gladwin, Francis,	The History of Jahangir, Madras, 1930.
Goulding, Col. H.R.,	Old Lahore, Lahore, 1924.
Grant, James,	History of India, 2 Vols. London, 1898.
Grey, C. and Garret, H.L.O.	European Adventurers in Northern India 1785-1849.
Haig, Sir Woolseley	The Cambridge History of India, Vol. III, Cambridge, 1928.
Haig, Sir Woolseley (Eng. Tr.)	Muntakhabat Tawarikh, Vol. II Calcutta, 1925.
Jarret, Col. H.S. (Eng. Tr.)	Ain-e-Akbari Vols. II & III. Calcutta 1891.
Jervis, T.B., (Eng. Tr.)	Travels in Kashmir and the Country of the Sikhs (Original in German by C. Von. Huegel) London, 1845.
Khan, Muhammad Walliullah	Lahore and its Important Monuments Karachi, 1964.
King, Sir Lucas (Eng. Tr.)	Memoirs of Zehirud Din Muhammad Babar, 2 Vols. London, 1921.

Lane-Poole, Stanley	The Muhammadan Dynasties, Paris, 1925.
Latif, Syed Muhammad	History of the Panjab, Lahore.
Latif, Syed Muhammad	Lahore, Lahore, 1995.
Lovell, A. (Eng. Tr.)	The Travels of Monsieur Thevenot. London, 1687.
Masson, Charles,	Narrative of Various journeys in Baluchistan, Afghanistan, The Punjab and Kalat. 4 Vols. London, 1844.
Mustafa (Eng. Tr.)	Seir Mutaqherin. 4 Vols. Madras, 1926 including Travels in India/Sinde and the Punjab by Orlich.
Nadiem. Ihsan H.	The Hydraulics of Shalamar Garden in Journal of the Pakistan Historical Society, Vol. XXXIV, Karachi, 1986.
Quraeshi, Samina	Lahore, the City within. Singapore, 1988.
Raverty, Major H.G., (Eng. Tr.)	Tabaqat-e-Nasiri. 2 Vols.
Stauart, C.M.V.,	Gardens of the Great Mughals, London, 1913.
Tavernier, Jean Baptiste,	Travels in India, 2 Vols. London, 1889.
Thornton, J.H.	Lahore
Tufail, Muhammad (Ed.)	Naqoosh: Lahore Number (Urdu) Lahore-1962.
Vogel, J. Ph.,	Historical Notes on Lahore Fort. Vol.I, Calcutta, 1911.
Vogel, J. Ph.,	The Master Builders of Lahore Palace in Journal of the Punjab Historical Society. Vol. III. Calcutta, 1914.
Vogel, J. Ph.,	Tile Mosaics of the Lahore Fort. Calcutta, 1920.
Wheeler, Sir Montimer	Five Thousand Years of Pakistan, London, 1950.

Lahore District Gazetteers
Numerous Volumes of Archaeological Survey
of India
Reports/Annual Reports.
And
Unpublished Notes.